GONE TO THE

TO THE

WOODS

GARY PAULSEN

GONE TO THE WOODS

A True Story of Growing Up in the Wild

MACMILLAN CHILDREN'S BOOKS

This book can only be dedicated to my new editor,
Wes Adams, and the whole team at FSG and
Macmillan. How joyful after all this time to
have finally found each other.

First published in the US 2021 by Farrar Straus Giroux Books for Young Readers

This edition published in the UK 2021 by Macmillan Children's Books
an imprint of Pan Macmillan
The Smithson, 6 Briset Street, London EC1M 5NR
Associated companies throughout the world
www.panmacmillan.com

ISBN 978-1-5290-4772-1

Text copyright © Gary Paulsen 2021
Illustrations copyright © Anna and Varvara Kendel 2021

The right of Gary Paulsen and Anna and Varvara Kendel to be identified
as the author and illustrators of this work has been asserted by them
in accordance with the Copyright, Designs and Patents Act 1988.

1 3 5 7 9 8 6 4 2

A CIP catalogue record for this book is available from the British Library.

Printed and bound by CPI Group (UK) Ltd, Croydon CR0 4YY

CONTENTS

Part I

THE FARM

1944

He was not literally an orphan, but he was a lost child. He was born in 1939 and his father was in the army – a low-level officer on General George S. Patton's staff who was gone for the whole of the Second World War – and they would not meet each other until he was seven years old. When he was four, his mother took him – dragged might be a better word – to Chicago, where she went to work in a munitions plant making twenty-millimetre cannon shells. She had grown up on a small northern Minnesota farm, wearing handsewn dresses made out of flour sacks and earning, if she was lucky, twenty-five cents a week. She now had a seemingly endless supply of pocket money from her steady hourly wage but was not even remotely prepared to resist the temptations of the big city. Caught up in a life of heavy drinking and wild partying, she no longer had the time or attention to raise the boy right. She didn't even celebrate his birthday.

Word of her newfound lifestyle found its way back to a small army of the boy's relatives in northern Minnesota. His grandmother was working as a cook for a road crew of old men – almost all the young men had been drafted for the war – who were building a road into Canada. A road connecting the United States to the interior of Canadian bush country was thought to be necessary in case the war dragged on or the US was attacked. At that time, no one was remotely certain that America was safe from invasion. The Japanese surprise attack on the Pacific Fleet at Pearl Harbour in Hawaii and, six months later, their invasion of the Aleutian Islands of Alaska were both still recent and frightening memories.

Grandmother was critical, then concerned, and finally horrified after learning that the boy's mother was not only going out more than was good for her, but was also taking him with her to bars, dressed in a small army uniform to sing on tabletops: 'Mares

4

eat oats and does eat oats and little lambs eat ivy. A kid'll eat ivy, too, wouldn't you?' Except his five-year-old version came out: 'Marezeedotes. Andoezeedotes. Anlittlelamzeedivy. Akidleedivytoowoodenyou?' The silly song he sang meant more attention for her.

He thought it was wonderful fun, because the men who wanted to meet his mother – a blue-eyed blonde who turned heads wherever she went – showered him with Coca-Cola and candy bars and fried chicken and hamburgers, all of which were hard to get because of strict wartime food rationing. He was, at age five, becoming something of a celebrity in the beer joints near the war plant.

Despite the fact that time is, of course, a constant, he learned it is differently paced at various points in life. When you're old, the years race by, but when you're young, very young, days and weeks seem to crawl and even stop. The period he spent 'working' the bars in Chicago, singing to draw men for his mother, lasted only a month or so, but it seemed a forever way of life before his grandmother – now past horrified and well into scandalized – arranged to end it and save him from a life, she felt, of degradation and waste.

The way she solved this problem said worlds about how the rest of his life would go. Her way of thinking taught him, early on, to deal with problems in a really practical, simple way: If it doesn't work Here, go over There.

His grandmother showed him this lesson the first time that summer in Chicago. His life wasn't working well Here, she thought, and she had an astonishing number of relatives available There, on farms in the northern part of Minnesota, not to mention that she herself was available to take him where she was, in the southern Canadian bush cooking for a road crew, living on a camp bed in a cook-shack trailer.

Simple. Problem solved. Get him out of the clutches of the fleshpots in the big city and send him to stay, in turn, on one of the numerous family farms she found available and, eventually, with her in the trailer in the cook camp itself. She ordered his mother in a short and tersely worded letter to put him on a train in Chicago.

And his mother obeyed. She dropped him off at the train station to make the four-hundred-mile run to Minneapolis to connect to a different, slower north-woods train that would take him north another four hundred or so miles to International Falls, Minnesota, on the Canadian border, where he would be met by a total stranger to take him the final rough distance to the first farm his grandmother had selected.

A five-year-old child. Completely and totally alone.

He made this trip during the height of wartime, when masses of people were moving around the world, across the United States; vast, desperate herds of soldiers and civilians shifting from city to city, coast to coast – going to the war, coming from the war, fighting *in* the war. Air travel – simple two-motor prop planes with limited altitude or distance ability – was virtually non-existent for the average citizen, and since it was nearly impossible to buy petrol or tyres or oil, which were strictly rationed for the war effort, travelling any distance by car was equally out of reach.

But railroad tracks went everywhere, which meant that anybody who wanted to move across any real distance travelled by train. Consequently, every train, no matter the day or the destination or the hour, was always, *always* packed with people. Short trips, long trips, slow hauls, fast hauls – it didn't matter. If you were fortunate enough to find space – because the military had seating priority – you went by train.

His mother took him to the station in Chicago, carrying his small cardboard suitcase. She pinned a note to the chest of his faded corduroy jacket scribbled with his name and destination, shoved a five-dollar bill in his pocket, hugged him briefly, and handed him over to a conductor. He was a kindly looking older man wearing Ben Franklin glasses and holding a silver hand punch to make holes in tickets, who assured her that the boy would be 'carefully watched'. As soon as his mother's back was turned, he jammed the boy in a seat between two wounded soldiers coming home to recuperate, and disappeared – he would not be seen again for the whole trip.

The boy was, of course, in awe of the soldiers and wanted to ask them many questions: Had they killed any Germans or Japanese? Did they know his father? Where were their rifles? But they slept, perhaps drugged unconscious by painkillers, the entire journey from Chicago to Minneapolis. He had to satisfy his curiosity about them by merely peeking at the bloodstains seeping through their bandages.

Although meant to be an express, or high-speed,

journey, the train virtually crawled. The distance from Chicago to Minneapolis should have taken ten or eleven hours to cover, but the numerous stops along the way stretched the trip over a full day and night.

In a short time the boy became bored, and then restless, so he pushed his suitcase under the seat, eased gently from between the two sleeping men, and set off to explore the train. He immediately learned that the cars were, in fact, a moving hospital. Wounded men were in nearly every seat, and many of them were much worse off than the two men the conductor had put the boy between. He saw half-body casts; shoulder and arm casts that made the arm stand out to the side; countless bound and leaking wounds; horrible red, shiny burns; missing arms and legs.

What he saw on that train was not the face of war that had been shown to the public. This was long before television, but there were newspapers at stands on every corner that reported on men fighting and being hit and killed. Every now and then they might print a picture of a dead enemy soldier, but the pictures were always 'clean'; tidy, intact bodies that could have been sleeping. The pictures in the newspapers never showed open wounds, eviscerated or blown-apart bodies, or burned flesh crawling with flies and maggots.

But here, on the train, was the brutal truth, the true cost of war. He was too young to understand much of what he was seeing. Even so, he knew that America was a big place, covered with train tracks and countless other trains, and he thought, if every train had this many wounded and shattered men, how could there be any men left to fight in the war?

Before he walked through those train cars, he had somehow believed that if any of our soldiers were unlucky enough to get hit, the end result would only be a small flesh wound that healed quickly under a small bandage. He had never considered that anyone in war could ever be this badly injured.

He staggered from car to car, dizzied by the overwhelming numbers of wounded men, the cloying smell of blood and wounds, the sickening odour of medical alcohol, and the dead tang stench of stale urine.

Finally, after moving through three or four cars, careful to jump over the clacking cracks between them, he found the dining car, where he smelt food, pungent and crisp, frying in grease, which could not entirely cover the odour of the wounded men.

He thought suddenly of his father. His mother had a black-and-white headshot of him on her dresser – which she would lay facedown when she was entertaining men – with his cheeks hand-tinted pink to make him look more alive. He wondered if his father was on a train somewhere like these men, and if he was alone and, worse yet, if he would be gone before they ever had the chance to meet. The thought made him violently ill.

He was huddled, retching, in a corner near the end of the car when a tall man wearing a starched white jacket appeared behind him, leaned out and over the boy like a living shelter, and asked in a voice so deep it sounded like thunder: 'What is it that makes you so sick, little man?'

'My daddy,' he gasped through the vomiting, 'he's in the war and I thought . . . he might be on another train like this somewhere . . . or hurt like these soldiers . . . I might never get to see him.'

The porter, his name was Sam, wrapped the boy in long, strong arms and held him, making a small sound, like singing from far away, soft and gentle, until the boy settled down.

'Don't you worry, mister man,' Sam said in a hushed voice, 'don't you worry long. Your daddy'll be all right, all right.'

The boy peeked at the porter holding him. 'How do you know?'

'I see it,' he answered, 'see it in you. You got the light, the right light coming on, coming in, coming out – shows all over you, so bright you could read by it in the night. Your daddy's going to be all right. But some of these boys . . .' His voice trailed off. 'Some of these boys are having to be men too soon and they need help. You want to help me help them?'

The boy had no idea what he was talking about, but Sam's voice was so soothing and his eyes were so gentle and kind that he nodded. 'I want to help.'

'Then here, you take this bucket full of sandwiches and I'll take this other bucket with the good juice. You follow me and hand out food to those who are hungry. I'll hand out what I've got to those who are just thirsty.' Then he set off for the front of the club car, and the boy followed him, gripping the heavy silver bucket with both hands, his stubby legs churning to keep up.

After they moved to the front of the club car and

entered the regular passenger cars, he went seat to seat to the wounded men and, if they were awake, offered them food while Sam offered drink from the good juice bucket. Hardly any of them wanted to eat, but many, most of them it seemed, wanted to sip from the brown bottle Sam carried in his bucket. A bottle just like many of the bottles he saw his mother and her guests drinking from in Chicago.

Many of the men smiled at them, but some did not. Those men seemed to not see at all and, especially if they sipped from the bottle, kept looking away, off and away, through them, clean through them, as if Sam and the boy weren't even there, as if *they* weren't there either, as if the train did not exist and nothing was there and never had been there and never would be there.

Years later, when he was in the army himself, he would remember those men and the way they stared. Only then did he understand the ripping, tearing, burning thought-pictures that only someone who has been in combat could ever know. The look they called 'the thousand-yard stare'.

Of course he did not know that when he was five years old. He saw only that they seemed to be in a daze. As he and Sam handed out the food and drink in the silver buckets and went back to the club car to replenish the buckets – the men drank up the brown fluid much faster than they ate the sandwiches – the wounded soldiers were so completely silent that all the passengers in the train cars seemed ghost-like.

By the third or perhaps fourth or fifth refill, the boy was so exhausted that he started weaving more than walking. He was not sure how or when it happened, but Sam picked him up, buckets and all, and carried him back to the couches at the end of the club car. He did not know anything else until he awakened hours later to a gentle nudging at his shoulder and opened his eyes to see Sam smiling down at him. He was curled up on one of the couches, wrapped in a light green blanket of soft wool, and had been dreaming of something that filled him and made him comfortable. Though he couldn't remember the dream itself, he hated to wake up and lose the feeling.

'We here, little man,' Sam said, nudging his shoulder again. 'We in Minneapolis. The conductor's got to take you off this train and put you on a different one. Open up, open those eyes, and see me.'

The boy was so thick with sleep and bone-tired that he couldn't wake up. His eyes closed as he felt himself being picked up and handed to another man – another older man like the first conductor. He carried the boy and his suitcase off the train and into the crowds of people flowing between trains. Set him down on the platform – even though he was still not fully awake – and held the boy tightly by the hand as they moved through the masses of men and women. The boy trundled next to him, staggering along, dragged by the one hand for what seemed an impossibly long time until he was handed to yet another man standing in front of yet another train. This was another conductor dressed in a dark work suit with a small, semi-military black cap, and he, too, picked the boy up and deposited him on a landing between two railroad cars, before climbing the steps and pulling him into the open end of the car.

He jammed the boy in another seat – alone this time as there were no wounded soldiers on this train car nor, blessedly, any smell of alcohol or urine – and covered him with a coarse woollen blanket, his suit-case at his feet.

'Stay here,' the conductor said. 'When we're moving,

I'll bring you something to eat and drink.' Then he was gone.

The boy was suddenly wide awake, and as he looked around, he saw that this second train was different from the first. The car was much older than the previous train and, though clean, more threadbare and worn, with cracked leather seats and worn spots through the rubber floor in the aisle. The boy would find later there was no dining car or porters – but the conductor soon handed him a sandwich and a small bottle of milk, which he ate in the seat in the passenger car.

Filling his belly led him to the discovery that the bathrooms at the end of the car – again, while sparkling clean – were not even remotely designed to be used by a small boy. Alert now, having left home nearly a day ago, and now with a full stomach, he needed to use the toilet. For many previously disastrously embarrassing reasons – usually occurring in the bars where his mother had him singing – he had worked very hard and become inordinately proud of being able to properly use the big-boy potty. So, after the conductor pointed out the facilities to him, he entered the all-metal cubicle full of confidence and pulled the door closed behind him.

But the commode was absolutely nothing like the toilets in the saloons or the apartment they had lived in. This one had complicated rods and levers and valves of shiny steel, and the seat was so high above the floor that he had to climb up, using the steel-covered toilet-paper roller for a handhold.

He stood, flummoxed, for a moment, but his pride would not let him go back out, find the conductor, and ask for help. And his stomach pointed out with urgent enthusiasm that he had no time for a delay of any length.

So he lowered his trousers, grabbed the steel toilet-paper roller like a mountain climber attacking Everest, and squatted. The toilet fixture had, of course, been designed for an adult bottom with adult dimensions and he was only five and small for his age. He did his business but then his grip slipped and he dropped like a stone down inside the toilet, jammed tail down with his shoulders against the back of the seat and his knees on either side of his face. Wedged in that position he could no longer reach the toilet-paper bracket – the only possible handhold – to pull himself up and out.

A sudden knock on the door brought home to him

the fact that he was not only trapped in a toilet, but also on a train with many other people who needed to share the one toilet.

The person who had first knocked politely, now rattled the handle of the door impatiently. The boy panicked and struggled harder, jamming himself still further in the bowl.

After a few moments of silent, frantic effort to free himself, the door to the toilet opened – thankfully, he had not locked it – and a soldier stood in front of him wearing a wool uniform with stripes on the left sleeve. The right sleeve had been cut away to allow for a shoulder-to-arm plaster cast that forced his arm straight out to the side.

'I'm stuck,' the boy said in case the soldier had not noticed.

'At least nobody is shooting at you.'

'Is that what happened to you? You were in a hole and somebody shot you?'

He didn't answer the question. 'Do you want help?'

The boy nodded and held up his hands.

The wounded soldier leaned forward, twisting sideways to clear his awkward plaster cast, and used his good arm to grab the boy's hands and jerk him out of the toilet. He turned away politely while the boy cleaned himself up with wads of toilet paper, hoping he would not stink of urine or worse, and pulled up his trousers.

'Do *you* want help?' the boy asked as it occurred to him that the soldier's arm might be as problematic in this small space as his own size had been to him. He wondered, too, if this was what it meant to be a grown man, helping another man out of tricky situations.

He shook his head. 'I've had plenty of practice now.' He waved the boy out of the toilet and the boy went back to his seat. The soldier did not come out for a long time, and the boy worried that maybe he did need help after all. But finally he emerged and gave a small nod to the boy as he moved to the end of the car, where he sat down next to a woman, his arm jutting into the aisle. They began talking in low voices and the boy could not hear what they said, but he looked very serious and she pointed once to his arm and then looked out the window, as if she were mad at him. Embarrassed at watching something so private, the boy turned away.

It was late in the day – nearly dark – and he settled back, not quite lying down, and probably would have slept except that the train stopped at every little set of buildings, shacks, really, that seemed to be in the centre of countless small farms stretching on either side of the train tracks. The train did not stop long at any of the stations, but, at each one, a number of people left the train – usually soldiers, both wounded and not – and other people came on, usually older women carrying dented galvanized-metal farm buckets filled with food they handed out to people on the train. One of the women gave the boy two hard-boiled eggs and a huge sandwich made with great chunks of meat on thick-cut homemade bread slathered with salted lard that tasted like butter, enough food to make two meals for a small person. She also gave him a pint jar of warm milk rich with cream, so sweet it must have had honey or sugar in it. He ate part of the sandwich and drank some milk, before screwing the lid back on the jar and wrapping what was left of the sandwich in some newspaper from the seat in front of him. Then he tucked the leftovers in the corner of the seat next to him, propped up so the milk wouldn't fall over, leaned back, closed his eyes, and was instantly asleep.

Even with the stop-and-go slow progress, the gentle

motion of the train lulled him into a deep, dreamless sleep. When he finally awakened, he was lying down, curled up on the seat, and had, again, been covered with a thick wool blanket as he slept.

The wounded man from the bathroom and the lady had left the train at one of the stops he had slept through, and he was nearly the only passenger in the car. He ate some more of the sandwich, drank his milk, picked the shell off one of the hard-boiled eggs, putting the pieces in an ashtray on the seat arm, and gulped that down before he turned back to the window and rested his head against the glass.

Although full and sleepy, he slept fitfully, dreaming of his father sitting on a train with his cheeks tinted pink, as they were in the photo – the only way he had seen him – even though all of the other soldiers were pale and wan. As the train moved north, darkness came slowly, a grey wash of diminishing light, as it always did in far northern areas. The country changed dramatically as the cleared farmland, with rolling gentle hills and tailor-cut bands of hardwoods between groomed and manicured fields, fell away, replaced by thick forest.

He awakened to full morning light and saw the trees

growing so thick and wild they seemed to crowd themselves against the railroad right of way, so packed together and dense it looked impossible to even push a hand into them. And green – as green as the colour crayon in the box one of his mother's friends from the bars had given him, trying to impress the boy's mother.

If anything, the train went even slower than it had in the southern part of the state, often stopping seemingly in the middle of nowhere. He would peer through the windows to spot a tiny shack or cabin along the tracks. There were many small lakes scattered throughout the running forest, and every now and then, the train would stop near a dock where one or two boats were parked, waiting to pick up departing passengers.

He awakened hungry and ate the second hard-boiled egg and another bite of the remains of the meat-lard sandwich he had kept. He had to use the bathroom again, but he proudly solved his prior dilemma with the too-big potty by going for arc altitude.

Back in his seat, he returned to watching the forest slide by. He saw several deer in the clear grass by the tracks, and maybe a grey fox or a scrawny wild dog, and who knows how many rabbits and, once, where the tracks crossed over a small stream, a black bear. The train was moving slowly and the bear didn't seem bothered, but stood on its hind legs to watch it pass. The boy thought the bear looked at him, into his eyes – or so it seemed – and appeared so natural and so much like a person that he wondered if the bear had a name. And if he did, what it would be.

Carl, he thought. He was named Carl, because the bear reminded the boy – with his rounded shoulders and brown eyes – of a man who lived in the apartment next to them in Chicago who was named Carl, whose breath always smelt like raw whiskey but who was always nice to the boy even when he accidentally kicked over his milk bottle by the door when he was running down the hall.

Carl. And because he – the man – had been nice to the boy even though his breath always smelt like raw whiskey, the boy thought the bear named Carl might also be nice, and he started then to like the woods, which were home for Carl the bear. In some way, seeing the bear made him see the other things in more detail. It was not just a forest, it was trees and grass and lakes and lily pads, and even though he was on the train and viewing the woods through the windows as they moved, he became part of them, or more accurately, they came into him, the woods grew into him.

He wanted to be in it. He knew nothing of the forest except for some painted pictures in books about fairy lands where small people lived sitting under mushrooms. And yet he believed, no, *knew*, that it was the right place for him. Because he could see – not just the forest – but each tree, and he wanted to touch each leaf and pine needle, feel the grass on his feet and legs as he walked barefoot. He needed to hear-see-smell-touch it all. The woods would be where he wanted to live and that certainty made him smile. And although he had been a little homesick, missing his mother and the bars and the men who bought him Coca-Cola and fried chicken and candy while he sang in his uniform, all of that seemed to disappear once he saw and knew and longed for the woods and grass and lakes.

He leaned back in the seat with his head sideways, happy to watch the trees slip by the window. But bone-tired as he was from the journey, his eyes closed, opened, closed finally and once again he napped until the conductor came to find him and picked up his cardboard suitcase.

He blinked, looking out the window – still daylight, the middle of the afternoon – and the conductor held out his hand to help the boy stand.

'This is where you get off,' he said. 'There will be somebody waiting for you.'

The boy was a little groggy, but the conductor took him by the hand and he followed clumsily after him to the end of the car, out on the small platform and down slick metal steps – far enough apart that he had to be helped down – and onto an embankment made of earth and logs. On the other side of this dirt and timber structure, away from the tracks, stood a small shack made of rough-sawn pine and on that was a plank sign painted bright yellow with numbers and letters: CAMP 43.

'You go stand by the hut away from the tracks and wait like a good little boy.' With that, the conductor waved to somebody leaning out of the locomotive side-windows at the front of the train. Then he climbed the steps, and with the hissing of released brakes, the train slowly started to move, picking up a little speed, before disappearing around a gentle curve into the distant forest.

Leaving the boy alone, in the middle of the woods.

But when he turned away from the tracks towards the little shack, he could see the end of a rutted trail through the woods. A small junk truck was parked – deserted, he thought – at the place where the woods cleared.

He didn't see anyone and he thought – even having lived in the city with thousands of cars and trucks, all old because no new vehicles were being manufactured as a result of war rationing – that he had never seen a vehicle so decrepit. He assumed it was an abandoned, ancient wreck left to rot. It must have been some sort of old-fashioned car, but the original body had been hacked, turned into something like a small truck with a wooden box-like structure on the rear. Old burlap bags and rubbish were tossed among rusty pieces of metal that stuck out at odd angles from the truck bed. Where there should have been a windshield, he saw a four-pane house window, tied on with what appeared to be clothesline rope. To cap it all off, the narrow wooden-spoke wheels were wrapped in faded rubber strip bandages.

The entire vehicle seemed to be made of rust held together by spots of faded black paint.

Suddenly, he felt intensely alone and desperately lonely. There was nothing around him but forest and the shack and the tracks fading into the distance. He was about to sit down on his little cardboard case and start crying when an old man staggered out of the thick brush to the side of the truck, pulling up a pair of heavily patched dungarees.

The Second World War had drastically affected every single aspect of life. Due to severe rationing, many kinds of basic food – sugar, flour, meat, and almost all vegetables – were virtually non-existent for the civilian market. Rubber was no longer available for tyres and tubes; petrol could only be purchased in very small quantities and only on certain days with restrictive rationing coupons.

The biggest fundamental change in American life was most evident by the absence of young men, mainly lost temporarily to active military service or permanently to the ultimate sacrifice. Women, and men too old for military service, were all who were left at home, so it was common to see old men working – driving cabs, collecting rubbish, and bringing ice (this was before many people had electric refrigeration and used literal iceboxes).

But the boy had never seen a man this old. He was bent almost double in an advanced stoop, his arms hanging at his sides, swinging ape-like as he shuffled towards the vehicle from the woods. He hadn't shaved in what must have been years, and his beard looked to have been chopped away with a sharp knife or dull scissors. The front of his chin – the boy could see this even from where he stood – was stained from spitting and dribbling tobacco juice.

He spit now, a great brown dollop, wiped his chin haphazardly with his sleeve and, seeing the boy, waved an arm hook-like to motion the boy to come across the tracks to him.

The boy didn't move. He wasn't exactly terrified – he had seen scarier, dirtier people in the city – but his legs didn't seem to work.

The old man waved again.

And still the boy couldn't move.

'You're Gary.' Not a question but a statement, and it came out as a raspy, gurgling croak.

The boy nodded.

'You're Gary,' he said again and then, 'I'm here for you.'

He spoke with a heavy Scandinavian accent, and mixed with the odd sound of his voice and the gurgling of spit, the words were nearly unrecognizable.

'From the second sister,' he croaked. 'I'm to take you to her.'

Spit.

'Eunice was the first, Edith the second.'

Spit.

Eunice. The boy's mother's name. Something familiar.

'I'm to take you to Edith. Come and get you in the truck.'

He knew he had an aunt named Edith. Although he had never heard her called anything but Edy, it was close enough to kick-start the boy into motion. He lugged his little box to the truck and pushed it over the wooden side into the back.

The car-truck had neither doors nor a back seat. The boy went around to the passenger side and climbed up on what passed for a front seat. There was no padding, just bare wire springs with a single layer of filthy gunny sacking for a cover. He could see through a bottom pane of glass on the makeshift windshield. There was no door to close, just a vast open space, and nothing to hang on to except the bare wire in the seat. He didn't think the truck would – or could – run, so he wasn't really worried about falling out.

The old man came to the driver's side of the truck, stood there wheezing and spitting, then looked at the boy.

'I'm Orvis. People on the route call me Orvis. So you can call me Orvis. They're far from here, Sig and Edith, too far to walk, and no telephone centrals up here, not even party lines for rubbernecking, so they didn't know when you were coming.' In all the time the boy knew him, this was the longest string of words he ever heard Orvis say. 'They told me to check on the route every day, and get you when you come.'

'What's a route?'

'Mail. I deliver the mail to the farms on my route. Used to be the Pederson boy's route, but he's gone to the war, and I took it until he gets back. Used to have a horse and wagon and a sleigh in the winter. But the horse got colic and died, so now I use my old truck.'

While he was talking, he leaned in and clicked a big switch on the dashboard, then adjusted two levers that were on opposite sides of the steering column just under the wheel.

'She starts hard when she's been sitting a time.' With that, he moved to the front of the truck where the boy had noticed a crank sticking out of a hole in the frame beneath the radiator. Orvis put one hand on top of the front end of the car, reached down with the other, grabbed the crank, and gave it a hard jerk.

Nothing. The truck sat silent.

He swore and cranked again. Again, nothing happened. He swore once more, louder this time, although the boy didn't know the words – he thought later, looking back, they were Norwegian – but he could tell from Orvis's expression that they were curses. Detailed curses. Vile curses.

'The throttle!' Orvis yelled, splattering the window with tobacco-stained spit and phlegm. 'The lever on the wheel pipe! Give her some more throttle, now! Push the lever up a few notches.'

At this moment, three things became evident to the boy. One, Orvis was – almost literally – frothing at the mouth as he swore at the crank. Two, the boy was afraid to the point of being terrified by someone who could be so insanely enraged over a car.

And three, there were two levers. Not just one.

The boy didn't dare ask him which of the levers was the throttle. Thought, if one lever is good, two should be better, so he reached over and slammed both levers to the top.

One lever was indeed the throttle.

By pushing it up, he sent more petrol to the engine. By jamming it to the top, he sent a *lot* more petrol to the engine. Way more than was needed to make it start or even run. Decidedly much more than it was safe to do. Enough to make the engine into a barely contained potential bomb.

The other lever was to adjust the timing of the spark that was sent to ignite the petrol when it arrived in the engine.

Which meant that two levers were not necessarily better. Indeed, two levers were completely wrong when jammed wide-open.

Which the boy had done.

If the timing of the spark is adjusted correctly when the crank turns the engine over at the precisely correct instant, the spark will ignite the petrol fumes and the engine will run properly in the direction it was cranked, moving the hand crank smoothly and safely and gently clear of the hand of the person making the effort.

And if the spark is only slightly out of timing, the motor simply won't start at all and nothing happens, which is what Orvis had faced when he tried to crank start the car.

But . . .

But if the engine is flooded with explosive petrol and fumes, as it was now, and the timing of the spark is hugely incorrect, say from jamming the timing lever upward, as it also was, then the engine will fire at the *completely* wrong split second, when the pistons are in the *very* worst position. The motor will not start and, indeed, an explosion on top of the pistons as the petrol blows will force the engine to run impossibly, powerfully, and horribly *backwards*.

Which it cannot do.

And much, most, of the explosive energy will be transmitted back down into the crank, forcing it to rotate wildly in a reverse motion with all of the slamming force of the engine into the hand, arm, and body of the person trying to turn the crank and start the engine.

The boy initially heard a sound – a *whummphh!* that shook the whole truck – followed by a large, deafening crack, like an enormous gun detonating. Then a shaft of fire shot out of the vents on the side of the bonnet. A cloud of heated smoke-gas spewed from the engine compartment, rising into a hot grey mushroom, and through this cloud, Orvis was airborne, flying through the smoke with an outpouring of Norwegian obscenities.

It turned out that the kickback on the crank handle had caught him stiff-armed so that the force lifted his whole body and threw him through the air off to the side into the weeds and brush, where he did not land gracefully.

His body looked like a pile of dirty, smoking rags with legs sticking out of it, and the boy thought, If he isn't dead he's going to kill me. He didn't know what had just happened, but he knew it was his fault. Because it was always the kid's fault.

For a long time the pile of smoking rags didn't move. But at last it quivered, shook a bit, and slowly – very slowly – rose to a sitting position and became an old man again. Then, folding from front to back, he rolled over onto his hands and knees and, without rising, crawled, clawing at the soil, up from the brush and dirt. When he reached the truck, he pulled himself to a stooped-standing position, all the while staring at the boy sitting on the other side of the front seat.

Into the boy's eyes, the stare, into his life and all that he would become, and past, way past his eyes, while Orvis gasped and hacked and spit down between his feet, lifting his hand, trembling, to pull the two levers back down to the middle position as he continued hissing and croaking, phlegm gurgling, his eyes boring through the boy's head:

'A little too much spark,' he wheezed.

Finally, in the end, the engine did start, and after much forward and backward manoeuvring, Orvis got the vehicle lined out on the road and moving along. But it wasn't like any car or truck the boy had ever seen. The top speed was about as fast as he could run, judging by how fast the dirt moved underneath them. And the vehicle did not run straight, but seemed to wobble, sliding of its own volition to the left and then back to the right in a gentle S-pattern. The boy felt like they were skimming over water. He would find later that this motion was caused by the wooden spokes being dried out and slightly loose, which required Orvis to pay constant attention to the steering wheel to course-correct.

That might be why he talked to the car. Sig – Edy's husband and therefore his uncle – told the boy later that Orvis had worked so long with a horse and wagon and sleigh, talking to the horse all the time, that he was used to urging his ride along in angry Norwegian. The boy thought, based on how he talked to the car, he must have really hated the horse, but Sig said you couldn't hate a horse. You could always, he said, hate a car. Because it had an engine, and engines would always let you down when you needed them – you hated the engine, and that made you hate the car. Plus they were noisy and smelt bad, and it was easy to hate something that was loud and smelt bad and would let you down.

The engine was so loud that it didn't much matter that Orvis was talking and swearing in Norwegian. The engine alone made a deafening *buckity-buckity-buckity* noise, and everything else on the car seemed to be rattling all the time and when they started up any hill – and there were many – the cacophony grew much louder as a growling came from beneath the seat.

'Come on, get on up that hill before I – no you *don't*, you stupid slab-sided son of a gun – you get *over* or I'll come up there and hammer you with a brick so hard cars all over the county will feel it.' And then he'd lapse into Norwegian, just ripping off words, spitting and hacking, clawing at the boy by the jacket to catch him when he started to fall out of the side of the truck, which was often, and then grab a breath, spit a gob, and pitch into it again.

The boy had no idea how far they had to drive. The road was not even a real road, just twin dirt ruts disappearing into the distance, or over one of the many hills or turns, so narrow the trees on either side nearly touched over the top as if they were driving through a long green tunnel.

The boy thought it must have been very pretty, but he had no chance to appreciate the view because he was always on the hair edge of falling out of the truck as it weaved, jerking in and out of the ruts. All there was to hold on to was the exposed wire under his rear, which did not help much. When he would start to fall, Orvis would grab the collar of his jacket with the clawed hand and jerk him back so hard he would slam all the way over to Orvis's side. Whereupon he would swear at the boy, the truck, the world, and then push him back and away so forcefully the boy would nearly fall out again.

And so Orvis would have to grab and pull the boy back once more.

Back and forth, back and forth, amid the *buckity-buckity* roar of the engine, the whining growl of whatever was under the seat, and a storm of swearing. Each time Orvis swore as he was looking at the boy, he would get a spray of spit that was brown and wet. And sticky.

After a time the boy could not begin to measure, they came to a lone mailbox next to the road where he saw another set of twin ruts going off to the side away from the mailbox, vanishing into what appeared to be thick forest. Orvis stopped the truck.

'Get out,' he said, spitting in the direction of the side ruts. 'This is where you are to be.'

'Where?' The boy could see nothing but dense trees and brush and even more of a tunnel than they had been through on the road. 'How far is it?'

'Not far,' he sputtered. 'Not far from here, but we cannot take the truck down there.'

'Why not?' If he was afraid to take the truck down there, the boy thought, what would happen to him, five-year-old, short-legged him, carrying a cardboard suitcase?

'The dog.'

'The dog?'

'He runs along the side.'

'Is he mean?' Does he, the boy thought, eat kids?

'He hates the wheels and runs along the side and bites the tyres to make them lose the air. I can't get new tyres until the war is over.' More spit. Gurgling. 'So I don't drive down there. Get out.'

The boy obeyed him – not that he had much choice – and went to the back and pulled out his box-suitcase. Orvis reached around to a canvas pouch tied on the driver's side and handed the boy an envelope. 'Here, take their mail with you.'

'What do I do?' The boy stood there, holding the envelope on top of his box.

'Walk down there –' he pointed one claw – 'or don't. You can wait here until they come to check mail, but they don't come every day. You might have to spend the night.'

Of course, the boy thought. I'll just spend the night. Here. Alone. Sure.

With that farewell, Orvis pushed the throttle forward, everything started snorting and rattling, and in moments, he was gone. The boy was surprised and a little alarmed at how fast he disappeared and how the slamming, violent noise so completely fell dead silent in what seemed like a split second.

For a very short time, the silence was absolute. He heard only the sound of his heart in his ears. But in another breath or two, the sound of the woods rushed back in and took over: frogs and birds singing, a soft breeze rustling the leaves, and things – sounded like something heavy – scurrying in the shadows.

He tried to be brave or at least choose the lesser of two evils: Didn't want to wait here so he might as well move down the side road. He felt tempted to run – panic being such a good motivator – but his suitcase made swiftness impossible and he stumbled along for what felt like forever. He'd only covered forty or fifty feet when he heard a new sound: a loud and most definitely life-threatening snake-like hissing. He looked further down the trail to see a lane-wide, enormous, rolling grey-and-white monster with wings sticking out at odd angles obviously coming to attack him.

He'd heard the soldiers on the train say there were times when a man didn't know whether to fight or run.

He had no such dilemma; he immediately dropped his box and the envelope and turned to try to run back down the path towards the road.

Two things stopped him.

First, the monster shape-shifted from an indistinct pile of doom into a visible flock of geese. The geese were clearly coming to attack and he was still terrified. But at least he didn't think geese would eat him, which of course an unknown monster would have done, as all unknown monsters always do. It had been in every one of the fairy tales that had been read to him – children were always being eaten by monsters.

Second, directly to the rear of the geese, he spotted a huge, shaggy-looking dog who, with a large bound, piled into the middle of the flock, snarling and biting left and right so hard he could hear teeth snapping. There was a wild explosion of feathers and goose poop (he could smell it) and while the geese didn't flee – indeed they turned on the dog – he kept them busy and, as Sig later said, when the boy told him about the attack, they made 'a whole life's effort of beating the tar out of that dog'.

Rex, as the dog turned out to be named, gave a

really good account of himself – judging by the quantity of feathers in the air – and it occupied the geese long enough for the boy to pick up his box and the envelope and make his way around the melee. He hadn't trotted another twenty yards past the dog-and-goose fight when he saw a figure coming.

Aunt Edith.

'Edy.' He thought how like a dream she was. That she was suddenly there. Just like a perfect dream. 'Hi.'

She was wearing patched dungarees and a sweat-shirt and a tattered straw hat, and she smiled so that her blue eyes crinkled at the corners. She held out her arms and said, 'Why, Lord, little peanut, where on earth did you come from?'

'Chicago,' he said, falling into the hug that was, right then, the most wonderful thing he had ever known. 'I came all the way from Chicago.'

'And how,' she said, holding him tight, 'was your trip?'

He looked at her face, thinking, remembering. Sick on the train, the wounded soldiers, the awful smells, changing trains for the run north, seeing the lakes and woods, people coming on the train with food and milk, warm thick milk that still smelt of cows in some way, being alone, no, *alone*, then the car-truck and the woods and smells again and Orvis, oh God, he thought, Orvis and the crank kicking him into the air with too much spark and being left alone, no, *alone* in the woods and then the horror of the goose monster coming to eat him and what could he say?

He took a breath and said:

'I got stuck in a toilet.'

HIS OWN ROOM

Their place, Edy and Sig's homestead, was a fairy tale kind of farm with a small white house with red trim nestled in towering oak trees. All the other buildings – chicken coop, workshop, storage shed, and a small barn – were painted the same way, looking like make-believe cottages the boy had seen in picture books.

It must have rained the day before he arrived, because chickens were busily chasing water bugs or finding worms on the edges of puddles. A sleek golden mother cat watched over her three kittens, who spent their time chasing the chickens and flying bugs. Rex, the dog who had attacked the geese, found a patch of sunlight and lay down on fresh grass. No sooner had he done so than two of the kittens saw his tail twitch and attacked it, which Rex didn't seem to mind. He kept flipping the bushy end of the tail back and forth to give the kittens something to pounce on. As the boy walked past him, he growled – a low, deep, stomach sound of a growl.

The boy stopped dead in his tracks. 'The dog doesn't like me,' he said to Edy. 'Why is that?'

She had been walking ahead carrying his suitcase-box, but she looked back, put the box down, and shook her head. 'It's not you. Rex is growling at the geese. He doesn't like them.' She pointed behind the boy and he turned to see that the whole flock had been quietly following him about thirty yards back. When he turned towards them, two of them hissed, lowering their heads and spreading their wings.

'Are they going to attack me?'

'Not while I'm with you.' Edy's voice crackled with a laugh. 'We've had a couple of discussions about who's boss, and it turns out it's me.' She picked up his box and started walking again. 'Come on, I'll show you your room.'

'I've got my own room?' He had never had a room. All he could remember were small, very small one-room apartments and sleeping on the couch. Or on the floor. In his memory, everything always seemed to be dark and grey in the places he had lived, even during the day, and there was never a thought of a room for himself. Mostly only the smell of whiskey and beer puke and tobacco smoke and the faint light through dingy blinds with the sounds of traffic and elevated trains nearby.

'Just for me? A for-*real* room?'

She didn't answer, but gestured for him to follow and moved into the house. There was a narrow screened porch that led into the kitchen and, inside the kitchen door, the boy was assailed by such wonderful odours that he had to stop again. Baking bread, fried bacon, milk still warm from the cow, a stew in a large black cast-iron pot with a meat smell he couldn't identify but which made his mouth water. He glanced around, taking in the rough wood counters holding two loaves of fresh bread the colour of new honey, and a pan of fried strips of smoky bacon above the wood range on a warming shelf.

The smell and the sight of food made him suddenly realize he was starving, but Edy kept moving through the kitchen, past the stove, and around a corner where a two-foot-wide staircase led to a second floor. She was in front of him still carrying his box, and the stairs were so narrow and steep that he couldn't see anything until they got to the top of the staircase.

There wasn't really a proper room; the space was an open attic with a dormer window on what turned out to be the east end – where the sun would come in every morning at dawn – which looked out on a shallow hill planted in corn about as high as the boy's shoulder. The hill gently rolled up and away and ended in a green wall of forest outlined in blue sky so that it seemed to be a picture painted on the window.

Next to the window was a single brass camp bed with a huge pillow and a thick quilt, both of which, he found later, were stuffed with goose down.

Next to the bed was a bedside table, and on it stood a little jug of water next to a glass. For him.

For *him*.

He sat on the edge of the bed and started to cry. Not crybaby sobs like when he'd been afraid of the goose monster or how Orvis had looked at him when the spark was too much. But soft, happy tears, barely wet tears. Edy saw and sat next to him and held him and he didn't mind that she was holding him, and she said: 'There's nothing to be sad about here.'

'Not sad,' he murmured. His face was against her dungarees and he could smell what came to be for the rest of his life the Edy-smell, an odour of warm sunshine and freshly baked bread and soap. 'I never had my own . . .' What, he thought, my own what? House? Room? Place? There, that was it. He never had his own place to be except under the kitchen table, where he would go when his mother . . . when his mother became what she was when she drank and had men from the factory over for a party. *Place.* That was it. He never had his own place to be.

'. . . water. I never had my very own water by my very own bed in my very own room in my very own house to live in.' He took a deep breath. 'Not sad, happy, just happy . . .'

They sat for a time in silence. Then out of nowhere his stomach rumbled and Edy heard it. 'Are you hungry?'

'I could eat,' he said.

'How about a thick slice of fresh bread with honey and a glass of milk?'

But what he ate wasn't regular bread with honey and milk. It was *warm* fresh bread cut in a slice as thick . . . as thick as the side of his hands one on top of another, coated with grit-salty butter and a complete covering layer of honey just gone to sugar crystals from a jar on the shelf next to the stove, and a glass of milk so thick with cream it could almost be chewed. And into the milk, to make it exactly perfectly right, Edy stirred a big spoonful of the same honey.

He took one huge bite and thought about God. He had never thought much about Him although he had heard swearing in the bars where he sang where they used His name. But the first bite into the honey and butter and warm bread made the boy think of Him and, when he chewed and it tasted so wonderful that it made his jaws ache, he thought that He must have something to do with it: the bread, the honey, the butter, how it tasted, how it all worked.

It had to be God.

He was going to say something about it to Edy but couldn't think of how to make the right words, how they would be, so he turned and smiled and with his mouth full said: 'Thank you.'

'You're welcome,' she said, and ruffled his hair with her left hand while she put the bread knife back on the cupboard shelf. 'As soon as you finish, we've got some chores to get done.' She poured a small bit of coffee from a large grey-metal pot on the stove and sipped it while he chewed. 'We might as well get you working right away.' A smile, then she downed the rest of the coffee, and they were heading out the door. She didn't seem to be hurrying, but he nearly had to sprint to keep up with her.

'Sig is out running ridges to scout for mushrooms and might not get back until after dark so we'll have to get it done on our own. I've already done the milking, but we have to gather eggs and feed the chickens and pigs.'

'He goes running in the dark?'

She laughed. 'Not really. It's just a way to say that he's working ridges. It's late spring, and the mushrooms come on the north side of hills and ridges, but you have to find them because they're not always in the same place year to year. And there's a full moon, so he can see to come home in the dark, which means he will work all the daylight he can, and that puts him getting home after dark.'

'What do you do with mushrooms?' The boy had mental images of the mushroom pictures he had seen in fairy tale books with the little people living under them.

'Eat them,' Edy said. 'We dry them in sunlight on the porch and they last through the winter and it's grand what they do to a venison stew in the middle of winter. It's like bringing summer into the stew when you need it most.'

'What is venison?'

'My, you ask a lot of questions.' She laughed again, and he found that one of the fine things about Edy was that she was always ready to laugh. 'Sig is going to get a kick out of that – the question business. He doesn't talk much – might go a whole day now and then without saying a word – and it ought to be a trial for him to keep up with your questions.' She took a breath. 'Venison is deer meat.'

He wondered how they came to get deer meat – he didn't yet understand hunting – but didn't want to ask more questions right away, so he let it go and followed her into the chicken coop.

A new smell – chicken poop and dusty straw – made his eyes water. Edy reached into a cupboard on the side and took out a bag and an old tin bucket. She pointed at the opposite wall that was lined with wooden boxes where he could see some chickens sitting. The chickens didn't seem to care that they were there. She handed the boy the bucket. 'Put a little straw in the bottom of the pail, then look in the nests for eggs and put them gently in the bucket. I'll be outside throwing scratch for them.'

He was only five years old and had never spent time on farms unless it had been when he was a baby, but he couldn't remember any of it. This was the first time he had been with loose chickens, mean geese, big brown dogs, and cats with kittens. All new to him, brand-new – as were the smells burning his eyes and making his nose wrinkle – but Edy seemed to figure he would know what to do. So he moved to the nest-boxes and looked in the first one and there were two eggs. Considering that he had never really known where eggs came from, it was like finding a treasure. In the next nest, a chicken was sitting and she pecked at his hand when he reached in towards her. He moved on. Next nest, three eggs. And so he went down the row. There were chickens in four nests, but eight more were open, and he plucked eggs from each of them.

Fourteen eggs in all. Again, just like finding treasure. He moved outside where Edy was calling, 'Here chick, chick, chick,' in a kind of song. As she called, she took handfuls of seeds from the bag and threw them out in a wave. Chickens came running from all over the barnyard to start scratching and pecking up the seeds.

'I got fourteen eggs,' he said, a little proud.

She nodded. 'There should be a few more.'

'Some of the nests had chickens inside. I didn't want to bother them. One of them pecked at me.'

Another nod. 'That was Yvonne. She's grumpy when she's sitting to lay.'

He had to ask. 'Why do they lay eggs?'

She looked at the boy for a long time as if she wasn't sure if he was joking. 'If the eggs are fertile, after they sit on them for a time and keep them warm, they hatch out into baby chickens – little chicks.'

Again he wanted to ask more questions – was it any egg they sat on to get a new chicken? What did the hens have to do to make the egg work that way? Why didn't *all* eggs make chicks? But he realized that he was asking too many things and besides, Edy was moving as she talked. She put the bag back in the shed and moved to the pig-pen, which was next to the barn, and again, he had to run to keep up.

There were two pigs in the pen. Edy handed him a pail hanging on a nail and said: 'Go get a bucket of water from the trough by the chicken coop.'

He had never carried a bucket of water from a trough, but again Edy seemed to think he would know what to do and so he went to do it. He found a big wooden trough, but water is heavy and the pail was big and by the time he returned to the pigpen he had lost a third of the water – mostly down his front – so she sent him back for more. Then she poured the water over the pen rail and into the pigs' trough. From another bag inside the barn door, she poured a thick grain mixture into the water in the trough, and the pigs dived in. They would hold their breath and keep their noses underwater while they snuffled up the slop. They seemed so happy, snorting and grunting bubbles, that the next new thing didn't bother him. Much.

Pig poop smelt worse than chicken poop.

And once more, before he could ask a question –
like why is pig poop worse – or say anything at all, Edy
set off for the house. 'Now we feed ourselves.'

He followed, nearly running, soaking wet and slosh-
ing as he moved. When they got to the house, Edy
turned and handed him a coarse towel and pointed to a
wash pan on a stand by the door. Another bucket on the
floor held clean well water and she poured some in the
pan and pointed to a bar of soap next to it that felt like it
was made of sand. 'Wash up. I'll have some stew on the
table when you're ready.'

He heard her slamming things around in the kitchen,
as she got wood in the cookstove and fired it up, and
moved the cast-iron pot over the hottest place. When
his face and hands were dry – although his trousers
were still wet – he sat at the kitchen table. As his bottom settled on the chair, he slowly realized two things.

The whole day – the whole trip and arriving and
helping with chores – was a complete blur. Like it had
happened to some other person and he could only see it
in pictures and even those were blurred. Added to that,
he was so exhausted that he was literally dizzy with

fatigue. He had trouble staying upright. Simply could not keep from sagging. He propped his elbows on the table, put his chin in his hands, and fell instantly fast asleep.

From then on, he remembered only snatches. Somebody – he first thought it was Edy, but she had a new smell, dark wood smoke and thick sweat – picked him up and carried him upstairs, took off his wet clothes, rolled him into a wonderfully soft bed under the quilt, tucked him in with a hand that felt like sandpaper. And then nothing but a dream about Chicago and his mother, which faded, faded, faded – gone.

He was not exactly certain which of the three things awakened him. There was sunlight coming through the window hitting him in the face, he badly needed to go to the bathroom, and the heavy sound of a man's voice came from the kitchen up the staircase.

Then he heard Edy's voice ask: 'Should I go up there and wake him up?'

Man's voice: 'Think what he's done, what he's been through. Let him sleep for now.'

'He didn't get any stew. He must be hungry.'

'He won't starve.'

'Small boys need a lot of food.'

'He's not that small.'

'Oh, you . . .'

'Oh, me . . .'

By this time, he was nearly peeing himself, so he got up, put on his trousers – which had dried while he slept – and his T-shirt. When he couldn't find his shoes, he thought, Never you mind, and went down the stairs barefoot. His need for the bathroom had become urgent.

The kitchen was bathed in sunshine – the same as his room (and he thought of it that way, *his room,* as if he'd been living there forever) – and where the light hit the table it made a big circle, like a spotlight.

Sitting at the table in the light was a man he had never seen. He would find his whole name to be Sigurd, although Edy, and later the boy, always called him Sig, and he looked . . . the boy wasn't sure then how he looked. In the rare times when Edy had visited his mother in the city, she was always alone – Sig never came with her – so he'd never had a chance to meet him before.

He had seen a lot of men in the bars who worked in the war plant when he sang, but they somehow didn't seem to belong where they were – they were always drunk or getting drunk and talking big and loud, whispering make-believe shallow lies, trying to get close to his mother – and they looked, in some way, out of place.

But when he first saw Sig, he thought Sig looked, no matter where he happened to be, like he was *supposed* to be there. He sat in the wooden kitchen chair at the wooden kitchen table like it was made exactly for him to sit there, and he held a steaming mug of coffee in hands that were nicked and scarred and looked like they were made of tough leather holding the cup like the mug had always been there. Always been held.

Grey hair, cut short in a bristle, and blue eyes that looked like they had electric power behind them.

'Got to pee?' He smiled at the boy, who was holding himself, trying not to wiggle.

'Bad,' the boy said.

'Go out in the yard and pee in the big lilac bush,' Edy said.

'Really?' He had never peed in a yard in a bush before and thought she was joking. They were both smiling. 'Really? Not in a toilet?'

'For now' – she nodded – 'the only toilet is the outhouse out back a ways, but I don't think you'll make it.'

Lots of talk, he thought, and the pee doesn't care whether you talk or not. When you have to go, talking doesn't work. Nothing matters when you really have to go.

Running out now, holding himself in a pinch as he ran, the ground sticky with something that squirted between his toes – mud, he thought, because it rained last night – but he didn't care, didn't care about anything except getting to that bush, warm mud squishing up greasy between his toes and finally, *finally* the big lilac bush, better than any toilet, closer, like shelter, like a friend, and the sheer wonder of letting it go.

When he was finished, he turned and saw that Edy was waiting by the door holding a bucket of water and a rag.

'For your feet,' she said. 'I didn't have time to warn you. The geese come in the yard at night to be safe by the house and they say nothing goes like a goose . . .' She trailed off and he looked down at his feet.

His toes.

It had not been warm mud squeezing through his toes.

Goose poop.

His toes, both his feet, were covered with grey-green-white, slimy, stinking goose poop. He had run right through it on the way to the lilac bush and had to make his way back to where Edy waited with the bucket. The poop literally blanketed the ground, and though he tried to half-walk, tried to miss it, tried to almost air-walk, he didn't succeed and gathered yet more goose poop on his feet and between his toes until at last he arrived at the step.

Edy handed him the bucket and rag. 'Get it all, dig between the toes. When you're done, come in for breakfast.'

It seemed to take forever but, at last, he set the pail aside and went back into the kitchen. Sig was still sitting there, sipping his coffee. He said nothing as the boy came in, but seemed on the edge of smiling. Not smart-aleck or teasing, but friendly, and the boy realized that both of them smiled most of the time. Or were on the close edge of smiling.

'Sit at the table.' Edy motioned to a plate laid next to a fork, knife, and spoon. From the stove, she stacked three small pancakes on a fork and slid them on his plate. 'There's raspberry-honey syrup in the jar; use your spoon to dip it on your cakes.' She used the same fork in another pan, scooping up three strips of meat that she slid next to his pancakes.

He didn't think there was any way he would get all that food down, but he was wrong. He couldn't seem to stop eating and, before long, had not only finished the pancakes, but the meat as well and a glass of creamy milk with some of the raspberry syrup stirred in.

'When you're done, wash your dishes and cutlery at the sink.' Edy pointed with her chin to a double sink at the end of the cupboard shelf.

He wasn't sure if it was allowed, but he was going to have to ask a question. 'Do I have to go out to the barn trough to get water for washing up?' Bad mental image: him walking, spilling all the way, through goose poop, falling down, in the goose poop, covered with trough water and goose poop.

'Use that hand pump by the sink. We have water right in the house. Did you think we were animals?'

He had not noticed it before, but on the right edge of the sink was a small red hand pump. He had never washed his own dishes before either, and it took him some time, pumping the lever to get water running, to scrape off the syrup residue and clean the milk stain out of the glass and, when he had finished and sat at the table again, Sig got up. He took his own plate to the sink and cleaned it and, without turning, said to the boy: 'Get your shoes on and a long-sleeve shirt, too.'

He knew then, knew a thing had happened, an important thing. Sig talked to the boy as he would talk to another man. Not a child. But a grown man. He did not say how to do this thing, how to put his shoes on or find a shirt; simply to do it. And Edy was the same. It's as if the boy were a grown-up, or more, even more, he was a person who was part of something. Part of a family.

They were, suddenly, a family, and he had never been talked to that way, as a grown-up, as a real person and not just a kid who somebody had to watch and take care of or he would break something. A kid who would do something wrong. A kid who had to hide under a kitchen table until things were better.

Part II

THE RIVER

THE CANVAS CANOE

'We'll take the river down to where it cuts those hills.'
Sig was talking to Edy. 'That's where most of the mushrooms were. They were starting to sprout here and
there. In another day, there should be a lot of them.'

The boy stood listening until Sig looked at him and
said again: 'Put your shoes on and get a long-sleeve
shirt.'

'How long?' Edy asked.

'Not sure. Two, maybe three days.'

'And you think he's ready for something like that?'

'If not yet, he will be. He must be tough, the way he
was living in the city.'

He went out the door and the boy assumed he was supposed to follow Sig, so he scrabble-tied his tennis shoes, found a shirt in his box-suitcase, and ran after him. On the porch, Sig stopped to pick up a roll of blankets and an old rucksack. He handed the boy the bedroll – which was nearly as big as him – and hooked the rucksack over one shoulder and was gone. It was all the boy could do to follow, the blankets' size and weight making him swerve and jerk. Sig was soon so far enough ahead that when he went around the side of the barn, the boy lost him.

He was about halfway through the yard-driveway in front of the house when the geese saw him and hissed and started for him, but Rex jumped in the middle of them so he could get away and scramble-stumble around the corner of the barn and out of sight. He saw Sig moving down through the pasture behind the barn. He was headed for what the boy thought was a long pond, but which turned out to be a small river that slowly wound its way through willows and tall water weeds past the farm and into the forest.

He would find out, many years later, that the river was between two wilderness lakes that lay fifty or so miles apart as the crow flies – which is a straight line on a map. But the stream didn't run straight and probably covered at least a hundred miles of travel to make the run. At the time, he wasn't thinking of where it might go but was hard pressed just to catch up to Sig, and when at last he did, Sig was standing by what appeared to be an upside-down boat that had been pulled out of the water into the long grass next to the stream.

It was an eighteen-foot canoe, made of narrow strips of wood covered with a layer of canvas. The canvas was painted with a thick coating of green paint to keep out the water. Here and there, a patch of black tar had been slapped where a leak had been, and when Sig flipped the canoe over, the boy saw two paddles lying beneath it.

Sig slid the front end of the canoe into the water, took the bedroll from the boy, and set it in the middle of the canoe along with the rucksack he was carrying; then he pushed it out into the water so the front end was floating. The back part of the boat next to where he stood was still on the ground.

'Get in,' he said. 'Pick up a paddle and kneel towards the front on the bottom – not on the crossbars.'

The boy thought, All right, here's another new thing to stack on all the other new things that were happening to me. He still hesitated, thinking that perhaps Sig would say more, tell him more of what to do. He had never been in a canoe or any other kind of boat, so he had no real idea how to do any of it.

But Sig said nothing, just held the rear of the canoe. Waiting. So the boy thought – what he would come to think many times as life went on – it must be all right because . . .

Because Sig told him to do it.

If Sig thought the boy could do it, he must be able to accomplish it. So he climbed in, wiggled over the top of the bedroll and rucksack, picked up the paddle, and settled on the bottom of the canoe. There was a lunge, a sliding motion as he felt Sig get in the canoe and push away from land, and then the canoe was floating on the water.

He grabbed at the sides of the canoe because everything seemed to wobble a lot and he felt as if they were going to flip over. But he looked back quickly and saw Sig was kneeling, controlling the motion of the canoe, settling it out by moving his hips back and forth to provide counterbalance.

He stroked once with his paddle and the canoe fairly shot into the middle of the stream. The boy's head snapped back and he grabbed again at the top edges of the sides.

'Paddle,' Sig said. 'Kneel like I'm doing and paddle.'

Easy, the boy thought, for you to say. But he didn't dare speak his thought out loud. He wasn't sure why, but he was fairly certain it wouldn't help if he started acting like he had in the bars when he had to sing and the men wouldn't be quiet. They called him a wiseacre kid when he bratted back at them.

For what seemed like the longest time, he was too busy to talk back like a brat. Just getting into a kneeling position seemed impossible without rolling the canoe over and falling into the water. And there was the paddle, which was taller than him by a good foot. When at last he was kneeling and tried to get the paddle over the side into the water, he dropped it completely and nearly fell in trying to catch it.

Still without talking, Sig caught it as it floated past him and handed it back to the boy. He grabbed it from Sig, but set it aside as he had other problems to deal with – starting with his knees. There was no pad on the bottom of the canoe, and he was kneeling on bare strips of wood full of sharp edges.

He'd also picked up a splinter in the web of his left hand grabbing at the side of the canoe. Kneeling, then half squatting in the bottom of the canoe, he chewed at the splinter with his teeth.

And, when Sig handed back the paddle he had dropped over the side, he had swung it around without thinking and caught himself a clout over his left ear with the hard wooden shaft. He could feel a lump forming.

He wasn't sure how long he'd been trying to kneel more carefully, chewing on his hand, resisting the urge to rub the lump on his head, feeling miserable – some minutes, he supposed – all the while Sig had been paddling down the stream until the boy suddenly noticed that the sun was no longer shining down on his back, but that they were in a green shade. At nearly that same moment he felt-heard in back of him a soft whisper: 'See. Look. See.'

It was almost not words, more of a touch than a sound. A hush of words.

The boy rose up, looking over the front of the canoe, and found he was in a different world. It was so beautiful that even later it was hard to describe, like an impossibly beautiful painting that by some magic had been made alive, *real*. As with the road and driveway, the trees had leaned and grown so much they touched each other over the top of the stream and made a green tunnel. And even that, just the way it looked, was filled with beauty. But more, because of the water, the trees had not only touched at the top but had kept growing, so that they were intertwined, making a lovely thatch cover, a long, wonderful room with a living roof.

And inside the space, inside the beauty, the stream slowly, gently slid along. On both sides of the canoe, lily pads leaned and danced with the current, as hordes of dragonflies moved from pad to pad catching flies and, sometimes, each other.

He looked back to see Sig, still kneeling. He had stopped paddling and was letting the canoe coast along. He pointed to the right with his chin, barely moving, and in hushed words again said:

'*See*, look, *see* . . .'

And there it was – the moment – the very split

second, of all the minutes of all the time the boy would ever have, that would never cease to exist. The moment – though he would not know it or understand it fully until he was an older man – when he would never again be able to, nor even want to, separate himself from nature. He had become folded into it; he had become an integral part of water and trees and birds and dragon-flies. The moment was so pure, so profound, that he caught himself holding his breath.

On the right side of the stream, just above the lily pads on the bank leaning down to get a drink of water, was a whitetail doe. He had seen pictures of deer and had seen them in passing rapidly from the train, but he'd never seen one in this way.

This perfect way.

Her coat was full and shiny and thick, coloured nearly red, and the hair looked as though it had recently been brushed and groomed. As the canoe floated into her vision, she raised her muzzle from the water and droplets fell from her lips like jewels to splash back on the pads in sparkling rivulets. She watched carefully, probably wondering what kind of log would drift by with two such weird limbs sticking out of the top.

The boy was so intent on studying her that he almost missed a fawn standing just to her rear. He – and he had no idea why he thought it was a male but he did – was staring at them with the wide-eyed innocence of the young, the way a puppy looks with wonder and awe at everything new.

Driven by curiosity, the fawn took a step towards them, so that his front feet were in the water. The doe, caught by his sudden movement and wanting to protect him, turned and nuzzle-pushed him up on the shallow bank into the willows. He blended so instantly and completely that he disappeared. The boy took a deep breath. She heard him breathing – they were that close – and it broke the spell of the moment. She turned away and vanished with the fawn into the willows along the bank. He heard Sig's paddle dip into the water as they pushed forwards.

They didn't say a word for what seemed like hours as they paddled. He was trying to help, though the paddle was much too big for him. All his pain and discomfort were gone – there was so much to see and try to understand that the pain disappeared – and the canoe seemed to grease along over the water in silence.

There was a constant flow of questions in his head and he kept turning to ask, but stopped himself before he opened his mouth. It seemed wrong to speak, to make a sound that didn't fit into where they were, what they were doing. The boy couldn't make it quite clear, couldn't articulate the feeling, the knowledge, but he knew. Knew it was special, and he stayed silent so as not to ruin the moment with noise.

And there was more.

More than that. Sig was there in that place, in that time because he was supposed to be there, kneeling in a canoe moving through this endless beauty, just as he had been at the table drinking coffee and smiling with Edy. And, by association with him, the boy was included. He was no longer the wiseacre kid singing in bars in Chicago chomping fried chicken and guzzling Coca-Cola, watching stupidly drunk men try to get close to his mother. He was here, part of this, a living part of what Sig was, by being in this place, being part of the beauty, part of the flow. Part of the joy.

And he was supposed to be here, where he was, who he was, how he was sure he would always be, to be here, to know here, to *be*.

To make a sound, to utter even one single note of a sound, would be wrong, would, in a very real way, ruin it.

So he held his questions and he thought, When it is important for me to know something, I will learn it without making noise.

MUSHROOM HUNTING

There were large flies around the man and the boy, only they didn't ever really bite. They would land to bite, but then buzz off without biting, and he watched and learned it was because the dragonflies would catch them – sometimes in flight – and eat them. One dragonfly landed on the front edge of the canoe, holding a fly while he ate it, letting the wings fall off as he chewed, then flew off to get another one.

They didn't hurry, yet the canoe kept sliding along, and the boy began to understand that, by being still and quiet as they moved, there was no line or gap between them and where they were. That they fit perfectly. As if the canoe had always been there and they – even the boy, not just Sig – had always been there, a living part of a living world.

They came around a bend and he saw another deer. This time it was a male, a buck, and his antlers were new and in velvet and his coat wasn't as pretty as the doe's and the fawn's. The buck saw the boy and Sig but, as with the doe, did not seem particularly concerned by the canoe drifting down the stream.

Sig made a strange choke-clicking sound with his mouth and tapped his paddle softly against the side of the canoe, and the buck, instead of being alarmed, seemed to get angry and aggressive. He snorted a quick blast of air and stomped his front feet on the stream bank. Then he seemed to grow in size, his front shoulders getting larger, and he turned sideways so they could see that he was bigger, and he snorted and moved away and up through the willows and was gone.

The boy had started making a mental list of questions – not to ask now, but maybe later when it was all right to make a sound – and he added the buck deer incident to the list. He had questions for later about the sound Sig had made, and how and why to make a deer angry.

There was a kind of spell about how they were moving. Magic. They did not seem to be actually going along as much as it seemed that they were sitting still, floating still, and the stream and forest were moving past beneath and above them on some huge endless roller, unmeasured streams of beauty sliding past them that would never end, never need to start again.

After a time, after a long time, the boy realized how exhausted he was, how completely dead tired he had become. He tried to fight it and paddled the best he could as one beautiful curve of water and lily pads with blooming yellow flowers and circling butterflies led to another until he found himself, without thinking, stretching the paddle across the canoe, resting his arms on it sideways, then laying his head on his arms. Just, he thought, to catch a wink or two.

Not really to sleep, not really. Just a quick doze.

And out he went.

He was not sure how long he slept that way, but he was awakened by a soft bump as the canoe came against a grassy bank. He turned to see Sig using his paddle on the bottom to push-swing the rear around against the bank so the canoe came to a stop sideways to the grass.

'Out,' he said, pointing with his chin. 'We'll set up camp here.'

The boy climbed out of the canoe, pulling himself up the bank by grabbing grass and willows.

'Here,' Sig said, standing next to the canoe, 'take these and find a flat place.' He threw the bedroll and rucksack by the boy's feet, and then pulled the canoe completely out of the water onto the bank while the boy gathered the bedroll and rucksack the best he could – a little clumsy – and continued weaving along the bank until he finally came to a relatively flattish place. As he looked around, it seemed to be the best he could do and he was about to point out that – along with all the incredibly new things happening to him – he had never before had to find a place to set up a camp. He had never camped. He had never –

He stopped. That was not a box he wanted to open – the list of new things happening to him that he thought needed explaining. Besides, that would be in the nature of asking a question – to bring it all up – so he dropped the bedroll and rucksack and stood there.

Waiting.

With the canoe well onto the bank, Sig stopped near

him, looked at the place he had picked, and nodded. 'Good.'

Then he gestured for the boy to follow him and they went to the side of the clearing and a stand of poplar trees. They weren't large – the biggest about the size of Sig's leg – and towards the lower end of each tree, the boy saw dry dead branches.

Sig broke one off to show what he wanted. 'These are air dried and good for a fire. Get as many as you can –' he smiled – 'and then double it. We'll need smoke-fire all night for when the blood drinkers come.'

Oh good, the boy thought. The blood drinkers come in the dark. Just fine. Silly to worry about what he didn't know when all he really had to do was get ready for the blood drinkers. This time he had to ask. 'Blood drinkers?'

'Mosquitoes,' Sig said. 'They don't take prisoners. They come thirsty and they come in clouds.'

He had seen a few that day in the canoe, but the deer-flies and horseflies had been the most bothersome. Still, they were not that bad, really. You could brush them off easily. But the sun was still well up and he was to find they would not become troublesome until after dark.

He was busily breaking off sticks and dry limbs for a fire, stacking them in a rough pile. He was never out of sight of the camp and he worked with his back to the woods so he could see what Sig was doing. He was setting up the campsite, but the way he was working, moving, it looked like a dance to the boy.

In smooth, almost greased movements he put the bedroll down, unrolled it, separated two wool blankets, and laid them on the tarp that had formed the outer layer of the bedroll. Inside the roll, an old large coffee can and two spoons had been packed, and he placed them next to a circle of rocks he had already laid out as a small fire pit.

From the rucksack, he pulled a saucepan, two tin cups, a large sheet-metal frying pan, a small jar of what looked like white butter but turned out to be lard, a smaller jar of salt, and a medium-size jar of what turned out to be dried, ground-up tea leaves. He reached back in the rucksack – it seemed to be bottomless – and grabbed a cloth bag full of corn-bread muffins. He rummaged again and pulled up a wooden spool of black fishing line that already had small lead sinkers and a hook on the end.

The boy had stopped collecting the dead limbs to

watch him. Sig looked up, saw him, and motioned him to come closer. The boy gathered what wood he had and brought it over to the fire pit and dropped it on the pile.

'We'll need more,' Sig said, shaking his head. 'But for now we've got to get some food.'

He pointed at the stream and waved his hand for the boy to come. 'You know how to fish?'

The boy shook his head and thought, Here's another thing I don't know, as Sig stooped, pulled a knife from his belt sheath, cut a long willow, cleaned off the small branches and leaves, then cut and tied a long piece of the fishing line on the end to make a fishing pole.

Just like that. Set up camp; make a fishing pole. Couple of minutes and it's all done.

'See those rocks?' He pointed along the stream at some small flat stones stuck in the bank. 'Go flip one of them over and grab a worm.'

'In my hand?'

He had a way of looking at the boy where he didn't have to say anything but let his eyes do the talking; and they were saying, Sure, in your hand, how else would you pick up a worm? Or maybe the question was, You mean you can't pick up a worm? What kind of person can't pick up a worm?

So the boy went to the stones, flipped one over, and sure enough, in the bare moist dirt beneath the stone there were several earthworms. He made a grab at one, but it slipped back down in the dirt. On the second attempt, he caught one in time – before it could slide back into the ground – and pulled it out and up.

Slimy, he thought, soft and slimy. He carried it over to Sig, pinched between his thumb and finger, and held it out. Sig took it, threaded it onto the hook, swung it out over the stream, and lowered it into the water.

'I'll do the first one,' he said. 'After that you can—'

He was going to say more, but the willow wand jerked down and he swung it up and away from the water and a fish came with it. The boy would find later it was called a sunfish – pan-shaped and perhaps eight or ten inches long with a fat, golden belly – and it flopped on the bank until Sig knelt down and took the hook loose. Then he handed the pole to the boy.

'Get a new worm for the hook and start fishing. We'll need at least eight of them, maybe more.'

The boy didn't see how he could possibly make it work, though Sig made fishing look so easy. But the boy had just spent most of a day trying to simply paddle a canoe. That he could catch a fish – or 'eight of them, maybe more' – seemed impossible.

But he got a new worm and, after several squirming tries, managed to skewer it on the hook while it squirted dirty goo all over his fingers. After untangling the line, which had seemed intent on knotting up, he moved to the edge of the bank and swung the hook out and down.

And here the fish took over. He had barely enough time to silently worry he would never catch a fish before one of them hit the worm and set the hook. He jumped back without thinking and wheeled the fish out and onto the bank next to the one Sig had caught.

He couldn't believe it.

But there it was, flopping around. He dropped the pole, ran to it, and held it down with his knee while he wiggled the hook out.

'I got one!' Hardly had he said the words before he watched in frantic disbelief as the fish slid out from under his knee, made two energetic flips, fell back into the water, and was gone.

'Had one,' Sig said. A short smile, then the look:

Can't keep a fish? Really? But then a different look, different smile. Kinder. 'I've had that happen. More than once. You have to get them higher on the bank away from the water or hit them on the front of the head with a stick and stun them.'

It was, for Sig, a long sentence and probably good advice, but the boy was into it now and he flipped a rock while Sig was talking, pulled out a worm and baited his hook, threw the line out into the water.

Another fish.

They bit nearly as fast as the hook hit the water. He lost a couple that wriggled off the hook before he could get them up on the bank but, in no time, had taken eight of them, and Sig almost laughed. Quick smile into a near chuckle.

'Easy,' he said, 'take it easy. We still have to clean them.'

'Are they dirty?' Really asked that, was honestly that new and a hair shy of terminally ignorant. He was not sure what he expected to happen, how you ate a fish or what you were even supposed to do with a fish after you caught it. His sum knowledge about gathering food was singing in a bar in a small soldier's uniform for fried chicken and potatoes, and Coca-Cola. He didn't think he had ever even come close to a fish, let alone caught one and eaten it. Although by this time he was hungry enough to eat anything. It had been a long day.

Another one of Sig's looks. 'No, not exactly. Here.' He reached into his magic rucksack – as the boy was coming to think of it – and handed him a large spoon. 'This is yours – come on.'

He selected a heavier piece of firewood and held and clubbed each fish, then hooked his fingers into the gills of four of them, motioned for the boy to bring the other four, and moved back down to the water. Watching him, the boy jammed his spoon into his shirt pocket as Sig had done and wiggled his fingers into the gill openings of four fish. They were a bit slimy, but he had been putting worms with black slimy goo from their insides all over his fingers on hooks for a while now, so a little fish slime no longer bothered him.

At the stream, Sig took one of the fish he was carrying, wiped it firmly on the grass to get the slime off, then rinsed it in water and placed it flat on the grass. He held the head tightly down with his fingers in the eye sockets and, using his spoon as a reverse drag against the direction of the scales, he pulled and scraped all of them clear until the skin no longer had any scales. Then he turned the fish over and did the same on the other side, rinsed the fish thoroughly one more time, before pulling out his knife and slitting the fish neatly down the belly. With two fingers, he pulled the guts out, flicked them well out into the stream, and stopped.

He looked at the boy. With that look where he didn't have to say anything.

With a small nod, the boy took one of the fish he was carrying, washed the slime away, put his finger and thumb into its eye socket – another new thing, fingers in eye sockets – and started scraping with his spoon backwards.

He did not feel that it went well, or easily; it was practically impossible. He kept losing his hold on the eye sockets, which seemed to be bulging out around his smaller fingers. Then, too, the scales didn't exactly jump off the fish, as they seemed to do when Sig was scaling, and he thought of swearing in frustration with some of the real corker swear words he'd learned in the Chicago bars. But he'd never heard Sig swear, so he held back.

Finally, after many scraping and wobbly attempts, he got all the scales off, rinsed the fish one more time, and held it out towards Sig. He didn't have a knife and thought Sig would have to do that part.

Sig took the sunfish, slit the belly open, and handed it back to the boy. 'Clean it out.'

He had already asked once, when he first picked up the worms, about using his hands – although the question came quickly to his mind – so that was out. He cringed at the thought of sticking his hands in fish guts. It wasn't something he thought he could be good at doing.

But Sig's look was still directed his way, so he reached out, took the fish by the eye sockets, held it up, put his hand into the guts, and scraped them out onto the ground and dry heaved – he hadn't eaten anything to puke up all day – right on top of them.

It was very quick and he thought perhaps Sig had not seen it, but of course he had and this time he didn't do the look, but nodded and said: 'Don't worry. Everybody pukes the first time. It gets easier. You'll be fine.'

He didn't believe him for a minute – was sure Sig never puked – but kept his mouth shut and accepted it as a sort of compliment, which turned out to be right.

The next fish was still difficult to scale, but seemed to go a little better, and he choked a bit on the guts but didn't actually heave anything up. And the one after that was still less problematical and by the fourth one Sig looked and smiled and said, 'It looks like you've been cleaning fish your whole life.'

Which wasn't true at all but made him feel good just the same and the boy followed him in a proud strut, carrying his four fish to the fire pit like he'd been doing that his whole life as well.

He still had no idea what exactly they were supposed to do with the fish next. Naturally he knew they were going to cook them and eat them, but he was so hungry he probably could have eaten them raw.

This was another chance to watch Sig work at living outdoors – to watch and learn. He made a grassy bed next to the pit and laid the eight fish in a neat row on the clean grass. Then he broke dry twigs from the limbs they had taken from the poplars, made a small twig teepee in the centre of the pit, and, with one match, started the twigs on fire.

As soon as the tiny fire was going well, he broke bigger sticks and still bigger limbs and stacked them over the little fire. In no time, there was a nice fire going and he picked up the sheet-metal frying pan, wiped it clean with another handful of grass, and set it aside. From the jar of white lard, he scooped out a good chunk with his fingers and shook it into the pan.

He then took two corn muffins out of the bag in his rucksack. Using the same finger, he smeared each of the muffins with a thin layer of lard, took the little jar of salt he had brought and sprinkled salt on the larded muffins, and handed one of them to the boy.

'An appetizer,' he said. 'Take small bites and chew it slowly.'

The boy grew to be an old man. And Lord knew he would eat thousands of meals in thousands of places from other great wilderness campfires and military foxholes to fancy, expensive restaurants in New York City where he could live a month on what the meal cost, but he would never eat anything to rival that muffin. Not ever.

He tried to do as Sig said. Take small bites and chew slowly. Edy must have used sugar, he thought, because the bites were so sweet and seemed to melt in his mouth in a salty-sweet joy-taste that made him smile, except that he was also close to crying.

'Good,' he said, 'so good.'

And he knew that Sig saw the tears but he looked away and nodded. 'She makes a great corn muffin.'

'Good.' It's all he could think to say. 'Way good.'

And it was wonderful, but it also had a downside in that it awakened in him an absolutely ravenous *wolf* of hunger. Along with the smile and tears, he nearly growled with it.

Sig nodded again, as if seeing the wolf in him, and he slid the frying pan into the fire and coals. Out of the magic rucksack he pulled a large potato, which he washed by rubbing it with fresh green grass. Then he used his belt knife to cut slices so thin you could almost see through them, which he dropped and spread carefully in the frying pan where the lard had melted and was sizzling. On top of the potatoes he sprinkled a bit of salt.

The boy's mouth was still watering from the taste of corn muffin and his hunger grew more pronounced, if that were possible, with the smell of frying potatoes. Sig used his spoon to flip the slices neatly over, like tiny pancakes, and in a short time he nodded and said, 'Done.'

More magic from the rucksack as he pulled out two

beat-up ancient metal pie pans and put them on the ground by the fire pit. He arranged the potatoes in two neat equal stacks, one in each tin plate, added a bit more lard and salt to the frying pan, and put in four of the fish, which covered the bottom of the pan.

The fish cooked rapidly and he flipped them over once to get both sides and then put two in each plate, using his spoon to spread the stacked potatoes across the top of the fish.

'To get the taste of the fish in the spuds,' he said.

'How?'

He had never eaten a fish, especially a whole one that had just been caught, and wasn't sure whether he should ask or not, but Sig nodded before he'd finished the question.

'Push the potatoes aside to eat after the fish, in case you get a bone stuck in your throat. The potatoes will push it down.' He ate with his fingers while he talked. 'Eat the skin first, then you can see the meat alongside the backbone and over the ribs. Lift it out with your fingers and eat slow and leave the bones in the fish. When you get done, you can suck the eyes out before you do the next fish.'

He remembered thinking that somewhere, some-place, there were people who wouldn't believe you could sit next to a campfire and eat the skin off a dead fish and then suck the eyes out.

And at first he was totally certain he could not do that either. But he watched Sig do as he had said, eating the cooked skin and sucking the eyes out with great relish, and he *was* hungry.

So he did it.

The skin was crisp and salty and made him think of a flexible potato chip and the eyes tasted like salty jelly. Before they finished the first two fish each, Sig had put the next four in the pan and they ate them and topped them with the salty, greasy potatoes, even though the boy did not need to push any bones down his throat. For dessert, they split another corn muffin in half and used it to scrape the bottom of the frying pan clean of grease and juice.

He was not full. He thought that he might never be truly full again after a day of only eating one meal, and so late in the day at that. But he was satisfied and more than ready to call it a day, to close his eyes and let sleep claim him.

But they were not done yet. He had leaned back in the grass and let the evening sun start to work at him when Sig stood up and took his plate and frying pan to the stream. He washed them, scrubbing them clean with handfuls of fresh grass dipped in stream water.

Sig didn't look at him, but the boy knew, he knew. He rolled over and took his plate down to the water and washed it, along with his spoon, and thought, All right, now it's time to take it easy.

'More wood,' Sig said.

This time he merely nodded and moved into the trees and started breaking dry limbs to put next to the fire pit. Only now he wasn't alone. The evening light had come, the soft time, with shade back in the trees, and with it came the blood drinkers, the mosquitoes. At first only a couple, then a few, and then, out of nowhere, clouds of them, so thick they plugged his nostrils and made him breathe through his mouth so that he wound up swallowing them.

It wasn't possible; there couldn't be that many of them. Thousands, millions, so many you couldn't see through them, so bad they coated his hands and face like fur. He brushed and slapped and slapped and brushed them away and still they came until he couldn't stand it and used some of the corker words from the Chicago bars while he ran out of the trees.

Sig was by the fire pit and he actually smiled at the boy as he ran up. The boy could see nothing to make him smile. But Sig shrugged and added wood to the fire and as the boy came close he threw a handful of grass and green leaves on the fire. A cloud of smoke billowed up, wafted around, and the mosquitoes disappeared.

Just like that.

'And that,' he said, 'is why we need more wood. A lot more wood.'

'But how . . . ?' He coughed smoke. 'How can I go back in there? They'll kill me, take all my blood.' He was already starting to scratch. 'Or I'll itch to death.'

'Stand in the smoke,' Sig said. 'Stand in it and wipe it into your clothes, your hair. Wash in it like you were washing your hands.'

'Wash in smoke?'

He nodded. 'It doesn't last forever but it will give you a few minutes until the smell leaves you. Then you bring back a load of wood and smoke-wash again. You'll be fine.'

The boy didn't really believe him, but he stood and did as he was told, washed in smoke. 'I'll help you gather wood after I get the water on.' Sig dug in the bottom of the rucksack and brought out the beaten and dented three-quart saucepan. While the boy stood in the smoke – he wanted to make sure he got a good dose of the smell – Sig went to the stream, brushed away a clear place on the surface, and filled the saucepan with water. He tucked it back into the fire and stood, washing his clothes with smoke.

'What's the water for?'

'Aren't you thirsty?'

He could have drunk the entire stream, he thought, but didn't say. They had gone all day without drinking, and if Sig didn't seem to need it, the boy wasn't about to whine. Once they ate, the thirst grew worse. The salt with the fish and potatoes had driven it into his brain.

'Can't drink the stream without boiling,' he said. 'Too much duck crap in the water. Makes you sick.' He gestured further downstream, then over to the left. 'On the ridge where we're going to hunt mushrooms tomor-row, there's a spring. We can drink there all we want. Pure water. No duck crap.'

The boy couldn't understand why they had to 'hunt' mushrooms. Seems like they would just pick them. But he felt he had used up his questions, so he held that one for later, with all the rest. Besides, they had moved into the trees and started gathering more wood. He found Sig was right. Washing in smoke kept the mosquitoes away, or most of them, and by the time the smoke wore off and they came back in strength, he and Sig had double armfuls of wood.

So back to the fire pit, more wood on the flames, more leaves and grass on the fire, more smoke-washing, then back into the trees and repeat. They kept going like that until it was dark and the boy thought they had enough wood to burn for a week. Huge pile.

By this time, he was so tired he was staggering, and when it was time to sleep, he didn't lie down so much as collapse to his knees, then roll over and sprawl on one of the blankets Sig had laid out on the tarp.

He did not remember closing his eyes, but he must have because he slept, or more correctly passed out, and dreamt one dream after another. In one he was being chased by geese, in another an old car was after him, and then the geese were driving the car after him . . . and on and on.

Sometime in the night, Sig must have covered him with part of his blanket, and he vaguely remembered coming slightly awake several times while a big bear – part of a dream – put more wood on the fire and added leaves to make more smoke. The bear had blue eyes and smiled while he put the leaves on the flames and then giant mosquitoes came with the geese driving the old car and chased the smiling bear away while he ran into the house through the kitchen and up the stairs to *his* attic room.

And then it was morning.

He woke up and the first thing in his brain was the thought that his dreams had been nuts. Who ever heard of a bear with blue eyes?

The sun was in his eyes and he turned away to see Sig sitting by the fire. When he saw the boy awake, he handed him a cup of water from the saucepan. The water was cool – he must have taken the pot off the fire in the night – and the boy sipped it at first and then, when he tasted how wonderful it was, gulped it down.

'Give me the cup,' Sig said when it was empty.

The boy handed him the empty cup and Sig filled it

again. 'Drink more. All you can hold. I've already had mine.'

Two more tin cups and he was past thirst, into hunger. Stomach growling.

'No hot breakfast,' Sig said – it was as if he were reading the boy's mind, or heard his stomach. 'No fire. We're leaving. Got to hit the ridge early.'

He was talking less now and the boy was beginning to learn how it worked, his talking. You could ask a question or help him do something and he would help you do it right, give you a good answer.

Just the once. And if you did it or it was obvious you understood what to do, that was it. He didn't have to talk about it again. And he didn't. Edy had said he might go the whole day without saying much and that's what happened this morning.

They rolled up the blankets and tarp, Sig packed everything that was supposed to be in the rucksack, they slid the canoe in the water, and off they went. Without a single word. The boy climbed in the front of the canoe, settled on the bottom on his knees, and grabbed the paddle. Sig pushed them out into the water, jumped in, used his paddle over the side to turn them and get them headed downstream, and stroked a couple of times with all his shoulder strength to get them moving.

The boy paddled as best he could and they went around two bends in the stream into another new world; more shade and, in this place, mossy banks so that it seemed like an imaginary place. He found himself expecting to see fairies around the next bend. But they didn't travel far. Once they cleared the second bend, the land went up and away on the left side, a hill that led to a ridge forested with poplar. Sig pulled the canoe over to the bank.

'We walk from here,' he said as the boy hopped out and watched him push the canoe over so the side was against the bank. 'Back and forth up the hill to the ridge.'

They pulled the canoe well up on the bank, Sig took the rucksack, and the boy came with the tarp and blanket roll – which was about the maximum he could carry – and they moved towards the bottom of the ridge hill.

Once there, Sig made his way into a small stand of hazel bushes and, on the other side, they came out on a little clearing with a trickling spring at one side. Here he set the pack down, fished out two cups, and handed the boy one. 'Drink all you can hold.'

The water was cold and tasted sweet, like drinking a sugared beverage, and he did as Sig said, sitting on the bedroll. Sig rummaged around in the rucksack – the boy thought, My God, is it really bottomless? – and came up with two empty cloth flour sacks. They had prints of flowers on them and had clearly been washed until there was very little picture left, but on the boy's sack along with the flowers there was a picture of a farmhouse that looked a lot like Sig and Edy's house. He had a quick thought-image of the house and Edy coming to meet him on the driveway and wondered what Edy was doing right then. It seemed they had been gone forever and he remembered with a start that they had been there yesterday and he had only arrived the day before that and he hadn't thought of Chicago or the train or his mother since yesterday. Or was it the day before?

Mother. He tried to picture her in his mind, but she came out blurry and edgy and he thought it was like a different world back there in Chicago, grey and grimy and stinky, and what if he never went back? How would that be? Maybe not so bad.

Sig interrupted his thinking by handing him one

sack and starting towards the bottom of the ridge, taking large uphill strides so the boy was nearly running to stay with him. After they'd gone a fair distance – the boy was panting – they came into the poplars where it was cool and shady and the short grass was slightly damp.

'They spread their spores in places like this, on the north side of hills in poplars,' Sig said. 'I worked this ridge the other day and found a couple of mushrooms. There should be a lot more now.'

The boy was still basing everything he knew on pictures he had seen in little books that were read to him, where tiny people lived under big mushrooms in a fairy land where the mushrooms were called toadstools. Which made him wonder why – did toads sit on them? And what happened to the little people if toads were always sitting above them on mushrooms and made poop? Wouldn't toad poop be worse than goose poop?

Or maybe toads didn't have to poop.

'What we're after are called morel mushrooms,' Sig said, again stopping the boy's runaway thinking before he started asking questions about toad poop. 'They're about as big as my thumb' – he held up a thumb – 'and look a lot like a little Christmas tree. They are also very hard to see at first, until you see one and then you can find them everywhere. Edy says it's because they know how to play hide-and-seek.'

'I see a mushroom now,' the boy said, pointing. It was exactly like the ones in the picture books – short stem and a little round cap on top. 'Right there.'

Sig shook his head. 'Wrong kind. Eat that and you'll die. Some mushrooms are poison. The morels are safe and that's the only kind we're picking.'

Well, the boy thought. They were hunting mushrooms and he found one, wrong kind or not. So.

'You go right, I'll take left, and we'll work up to the top of the ridge.' He started moving, only not big strides but careful, like he was actually hunting something alive. The boy did the same, careful of the way he moved, watching the ground, and for fifteen or twenty steps he saw nothing but green grass.

'Like this,' Sig said in a moment. 'Come see.'

As the boy came up to him, he held out a small dark mushroom, and he was right. It was about three inches high, brown and tapered with little ridges running up and down the side looking for all the world like a tiny brown Christmas tree.

'Look for this,' he said. 'See the shape of the line? If you look for that shape, the little cone shape, it makes them easier to see.'

The boy moved off to the side and started up the hill. At first he saw many of the other kind of mushroom – the toadstools – but none of the morels. And then, at the base of a tree, near a coating of moss, he saw one. It seemed to appear, as if by magic – as so many things seemed magical lately – just there. No mushroom, and then a mushroom.

'I found one,' he yelled to Sig. 'How do I pick it?'

'Take it all. The top and the stem. Just take it up and put it in your sack and look for more . . .'

He picked it – it came away easily – and put it in his flour bag and stood, and again, as if by some change in light or shade, he saw them all over the place. It didn't seem possible. He had looked before and didn't see any and now they were everywhere and he went to picking.

He could not have measured time or even distance. He kept picking what he could see and moving to the next stand, sticking them in his flour sack as he went. He was completely caught up hunting, his head down, looking for the next mushroom, perhaps halfway to the top of the ridge, when Sig called to him.

'Wait for a second.'

He had been working well away from the boy's position, and now he set his sack down and took long strides over to him. From inside his shirt pocket, he dug out a corn muffin and handed it to the boy.

'Put it in your shirt pocket and, every so often, take small bites and let them soak in your mouth without chewing before you swallow. It will keep you going.'

No questions. The boy did exactly as he said, and Sig was right. He would pull the muffin out of his pocket, take a tiny bite, tuck it into his cheek, being sure to not let any crumbs on his hand or in the pocket go to waste, and move up the hill, picking mushrooms as they came.

And they came fast. They were like a giant rug of little Christmas trees, and about the time they got to the top of the ridge, two things occurred to him. His sack was full. Right to the top. And his back and legs were tired and his joints were aching, burning.

Sig walked over. His sack was also full, but he didn't look particularly tired.

'We've got a problem,' he said, smiling the short smile, eyes crinkled.

The boy nodded. 'I'm exhausted.'

He shook his head. 'More than that – too many mushrooms. I've never seen them this thick. Usually we might get one bag or so. Now we're already full up on what we need – full and more.'

'Why is that a problem?' A question, he thought. I shouldn't have asked – he'll tell without asking.

'We used to try and dry some on the tarp spread on the ground while we kept picking. Now, though, we have to head home as fast as we can so Edy can get them to drying on protected racks in the porch.'

He stopped himself from asking why, why, why . . .

'There's too many for the tarp and if we put the extras off in the dirt to dry they'll spoil or the ants will get them. We have to go. Head back. Right away.'

It was downhill back to the canoe and took them only a few minutes to get there. They put the mushroom sacks in the middle with the bedroll and rucksack, the boy climbed in the front and knelt on the bottom as Sig jumped in, pushed them out into the stream, and they started back.

They were paddling upstream, which slowed them a bit, but there was virtually no current, and though it was late in the day, they covered a good distance before dark set in.

The boy paddled as well as he could, catching a good stroke now and again, but Sig kept up a strong push all the time.

As the sun went down, the mosquitoes came up. They kept moving away from them for a while, but soon the mosquitoes caught up with them and were clouded around the canoe so thick, it was hard to breathe without getting a mouthful.

Finally, Sig said a couple of words the boy had heard in the bars in Chicago and steered the canoe to shore near some dead willows. Without getting out, he broke off some dry sticks, carefully fashioned them into short pieces. Next he took the saucepan out of the pack and put it on the floorboards of the canoe. He put some river mud in the bottom of the pan, maybe an inch thick, then stacked dry sticks on top of the mud, lit them with a match, and as soon as they were going well, he grabbed a handful of green grass and some leaves off live willows and threw them on top of the flames.

Instant smoke.

No mosquitoes.

Just that fast.

Sig pushed the canoe out into the stream again and they kept moving. The smoke swirled and worked around them in the canoe as they paddled. Now and then it got in his eyes or made him sneeze, but that was much better than the – he thought – evil mosquitoes.

They had paddled a large part of the day to get to the campsite, and then more the next morning. Plus, that had been with the current. They were now going back against it, and while it wasn't very strong, it was enough to slow them a bit and make it more difficult to paddle.

First it was evening, and the mosquitoes, but soon after that came the hard dark, and for a time, he couldn't see much past the front of the canoe. But before long the moon came up – first a glow over the trees and then full-on white and bright. It shone on the stream ahead of them and made the water look like silver, and for a time, he was caught by the beauty of it. There were so many things happening to him now that he had never seen before that it seemed to fill his brain with new pictures, new sounds, new smells.

Yet, pretty or not, silver or not, new or not, they

had to keep paddling. And though he couldn't come anywhere close to what Sig was doing, he did the best he could, and before long, his arms hurt, his shoulders ached, and his knees where he knelt on the floorboards seemed to be on fire.

But it didn't matter that there was aching or pain.

Keep paddling.

Had to keep moving.

In a short time for the boy – if not for Sig – it seemed they were not moving at all. They stroked the paddle forward and pulled it back and then again and again and again.

And again.

Up the silver path on the water, except that it seemed the silver was coming towards them, not that they were moving towards the path, and then, in the end, nothing.

Just arms and paddles and back and knees and shoulders and smoke from the mosquito fire and exhaustion, so bone-tired that he couldn't even tell when or if his eyes closed. No lying down on the cross boards this time, no peaceful dozing off into dreamland.

Just nothing.

Maybe not even sleep so much as an absence of

thought, a going away of his mind, a stopping of all things; he went out and into some greyness and then a dark hole that formed around him, and still kneeling, without going physically down, his body simply quit.

He could not tell about the rest of that night. Small nudges of memory, little quick images: Sig pulling to the shore for more twigs and grass to make smoke, hour after hour of the canoe sliding under him, then bumping gently against the bank, being pulled onto shore still in the canoe, Edy's higher voice, soft and gentle, the dog whining, being carried by Sig, the boy's cheek against his coarse whiskers, past the barn into the kitchen up the stairs and into bed.

The bed in *his* room, and then only deep wonderful sleep.

JOBS OF WORK AND HORSE SLEEP

After hunting mushrooms and coming back to the farm, he worked with both Edy and Sig at whatever they were doing, depending on who wanted him. Sometimes with both at the same time.

He helped Edy spread the mushrooms to dry on racks covered with sheets in the porch, and found that he had certain jobs of work – that's how Sig put it – 'you've got particular jobs of work to do'. Not just slapping mushrooms on the drying racks. Each mushroom had to be shaken free of dirt, and any extra soil at the base needed to be cleaned off before the morel could be carefully placed on the drying surface where the afternoon sun could get at it. It didn't sound like much and it didn't tire him, but the work took time and had to be done right or the mushrooms would spoil and not be there in winter for soup and stew.

There were other jobs of work as well.

He couldn't split wood for the stove. The axe was a big double-bladed Collins so sharp Sig could shave arm hair with it, too heavy for the boy to handle. He tried, but it looked like if he didn't handle it right, it would take off his foot or at least a toe – that's how Edy put it – so he had to back away from splitting.

His job of work with wood was to carry it into the house each morning and fill the woodbox behind the cookstove. He also gathered sticks and chips for Edy to use for kindling to start the stove if the coals went cold in the night, which they usually did, and he was surprised at how much wood it took to bake bread or cook pancakes or brew coffee. He started to drink coffee about then. Not a lot, and Sig added a good dollop of cold water to his cup, and the boy took it with milk and honey, two spoons, but every morning before starting the morning chores they would have a 'bite of coffee', is how Sig put it, and maybe one or two biscuits.

Then they would milk. They had three cows, but only milked one, which gave plenty of milk, way more than they needed. He couldn't actually milk. His hands were too small for the teats, which hung down like little handles or miniature milk hoses. He tried it and got a tiny bit to squirt into a waiting kitten's mouth, but because his hands didn't fit right, Edy said it might cause the cow to be upset and stop giving milk and there would be no cream, butter, and drinking milk. So his job of work with the milking was to go out in the pasture with Rex and bring the cows into the barn to get milked.

There would be many favourite parts of his staying with Edy and Sig, many things that would make him think happiness thoughts as time passed. But going for the cows morning and evening was one of the best of all times.

The cows kept the pasture grazed down so that it looked like one beautiful, giant manicured lawn. Birds that Sig called killdeers ranged all over, catching bugs from the spots of manure left by the cows. Some of them had baby chicks and the mothers would work, moving away from them pretending to have a broken wing, trying to lead Rex and the boy away from the babies' nest. When they had lured the dog and the boy a distance they figured to be far enough to protect the chicks, they would suddenly be 'cured' and fly off, still away from the chicks as a ruse, before finally circling back.

He would have and be had by many dogs in his life, but Rex was, he thought, unique. He was, by definition, a yard dog. When they went off in the canoe, for instance, he did not try to follow along the bank, which many dogs would do, but stayed with the house, the yard. He went with the boy to get the cows, into the nearby pasture, but only that far. Any other time he stayed in the yard, around the house – and he *ruled* the yard. He would position himself where he could see every part of the house, barn, sheds, and yard and stay there, watching everything, studying everything. And if he saw something out of kilter, something not quite right – like the two tomcats fighting, which happened now and again, or the geese coming after the boy, or anything, absolutely *anything* bothering the chickens – he would step in and end the problem. He once caught a skunk trying to get into the chicken pen, and he literally tore it to pieces. Stinking pieces. God-awful thick-stinking pieces all over the yard and they couldn't get close to Rex for over a week from the smell on him, but that skunk didn't, and never would, get at any chickens.

They really didn't have to bring the cows in. When it was time to milk, the cows would start by themselves to head to the barn, but walking out to them, walking in after them, in that beautiful huge green trimmed lawn with killdeer flying around and Rex walking softly by his side was like being in a world made just for him to enjoy.

He would take his shoes off when he hit the pasture and hang them around his neck by the shoelaces and walk barefoot in the damp green grass, wiggling his toes when the blades tickled him. Now and then if he wasn't paying attention – usually because he was being led away by killdeer mothers – he would accidentally step in fresh cow poop. It was sticky, squirting between his toes, but somehow not as bad as goose poop. Couldn't explain why, just not as bad, and washed out cleaner in the stream.

In the centre of the pasture, there was a salt block the cows licked, making curved, gouged-out pockets in the salt. They made it look so good he tried it a few times. Coarse salt taste, but not bad, and sometimes, when he went for the cows in the afternoons when the sun was hot, it tasted downright good.

They seemed to know things, the cows. They would walk along ahead of Rex and him, almost as if they were lost in thought, walking slowly on the path that led to the barn. Sometimes the boy would walk next to their shoulders and put his hand on them, thinking, he didn't know, that he might learn something that they knew by touching them. Felt good, made him feel good inside, but he couldn't tell why, and they didn't seem to mind.

When they got to the barn, they went in by themselves, climbed into their own stalls, and stood while the boy went to the feed sack and gave them each a scoop full of something Edy called 'sweet feed' grain in their lick-shaped, worn-wood feed boxes. Like the salt block, they made it look so good he tried a bit, chewing it slowly. It wasn't bad. Sort of sweet, a treacle-and-iron taste, and he thought he might try it in a bowl with milk and honey, but he never got around to it at breakfast. Too much other good stuff – pancakes with raspberry syrup, mush with a dollop of salty lard in the middle and dripped over with honey from the partially sugared honey jar, salt-cured bacon so crisp it broke in pieces, eggs from the coop with the bacon – for him to get into animal feed. But there would be times in his life later, in the army, in hard-hungry places when he would remember that cow sweet feed with fond memories.

Getting the cows in twice a day wasn't all the cow work. His job of work after that was to shovel clean the gutter. While the cows weren't in the barn that long – just for milking – and then went back out to pasture, they would almost always leave what Sig called 'a perfect present' in the gutter. Wet, flop-wet, plop-wet, if he was close when they dropped it – it fell about four feet into the gutter – it was impossible to keep from getting the splatter on him somewhere. Sometimes in his face, and sometimes a bit might go in his mouth. Not the absolute worst thing in the world, but he spit pretty regular until he could find a new taste to take over. Maybe a lick of salt or spoonful of honey. There were lots of things that tasted better than cow poop.

When milking was finished, the milk was put in tall can-buckets and carried to the well house, next to the chicken coop. Down in the well some feet was a shelf-ledge where the temperature stayed lower than outside and the bottoms of the tall milk containers were actually in the water for half a foot or so, which kept them especially cool. Any extra milk left from before – and there was always a good amount – was put outside in a low wood trough for the chickens. Edy said it made their shells stronger and the eggs taste better, which was true by him since he thought they tasted great. Especially with crisp bacon and fresh baked bread toasted on the flat of the woodstove top.

He noticed that the chickens weren't the only things to hit the milk trough. The kittens licked at it until the sun made it sour, and even then he caught Rex licking at it a few times, not to mention now and then blue jays would fly in and take a little.

After milking chores were done and the barn gutters cleaned, his job of work was to gather eggs in the old bucket with straw in the bottom and throw some feed out in the dirt for the chickens to scratch at and eat.

Then to the house, wash his hands and face at the washstand, wipe them on the towel hanging on an old deer antler nailed to the wall above the sink, and in to breakfast, which was mush with lard and salt and honey or pancakes or eggs and fresh bread (Sig called it 'new' bread). Eat until he thought he was going to pop. And, of course, coffee.

After breakfast, it was time to get into the work of the day.

The garden was a large plot in back of the house, to the rear of the outhouse, which needed to be constantly weeded – especially the part with the new potatoes, because they had been planted early, and the three rows of sweet corn. Sig said corn was a weak plant and that the weeds would kill it if you didn't keep it clean. So the way it worked was – no matter who you were – anytime you weren't doing anything else, you'd go back and have a go at weeding the garden with the hoe kept as sharp as the axe, or pull the weeds out by hand so you get the roots.

He hated weeds his whole life because of that garden plot.

Bloody things. Heard Edy say that once, so he picked it up.

Bloody things.

Weeds.

When he'd been there long enough to get into the rhythm of things and knew his own jobs of work – and if he took in weeding the garden along with the rest of the other morning and afternoon chores, it took most of a day. One morning after breakfast Sig looked across the table at him and said: 'We've got to cultivate the cornfield today.'

There was corn in the garden, weeded so often he didn't think there was a single bad plant there. But that was sweet corn, roasting corn. What Edy called table corn. The other was field corn, which the boy knew, or thought he knew, was mainly for animal feed. It was quite a large field – he supposed later in memory it might have been twenty or so acres – and much too large to weed by hand.

Plus he had said 'cultivate,' which the boy did not exactly understand, but he sat quiet. He had learned a lot from Sig, and the one most important thing was if you didn't bother him with questions you would sooner or later get the answer. Mostly sooner. So the word 'cultivate' he filed in his not-know corner for the moment.

'Which means the horses,' he said, finishing his coffee. 'We've got to get them in from the pasture.'

' "We"?' he said. 'You mean you want me to help get the horses?'

Which posed a problem. They were in the same pasture as the cows, usually away from them, way down at the east end where they stood in the shade of some fence elms. They typically didn't come into the barn, just drank water from the stream, and ignored the boy as much as he ignored them.

It wasn't that he was particularly afraid of them. Merely thoughtful of how they ignored him. And they were so enormous, easily twice as large as the cows, like one brown and one tan hair-covered walls on legs – he thought that he could have walked under them – that it was more sensible to kind of, well, let them be.

'You can bring them in,' Sig said, making the boy's brain go blank. 'I'll grease the cultivator and get the harnesses ready while you go get them.'

Sure, he thought, no problem. Been doing this all my life. 'How do I do that?'

'Just take a lead rope off those pegs in the west end of the barn, go out, and put it around one of their necks and lead him in – doesn't matter which one, the other will follow.'

What, he thought, if they didn't want to come? What if one of them stepped on him? But he kept his mouth shut, and resigned to his possible fate, made his way to the barn. Their feet were as big as wash-tubs, he thought as he headed closer to them. He'd be smashed to goo in the pasture. What if that happened? How could you even pick up kid goo? With a shovel? A mop? Was it ploppy like cow poop? Smelly like goose poop?

He picked up a lead rope and walked out of the barn. The horses were both down at the end of the pasture where they usually stayed, and he made his way but did not exactly hurry – carefully studying killdeers and green grass and almost everything else in the world as he did not exactly hurry – towards them.

When he was in the pasture, they largely – and 'largely' is the word – ignored him. This time when they saw him coming though, they grew more alert – Sig said later it was because they saw he was holding the lead rope – and started towards him. And then the brown one – he found later his name was Jim – broke into a shambling trot.

Heading straight for the boy.

And the other one – named Blackie – picked up the trot, too, and they seemed to be moving faster as he watched, covering an amazing amount of ground with each giant foot that came down. Their trot sounded like small thunder. Not so small, though.

Straight at him.

He stopped. He had absolutely no idea what he should do. Running seemed out of the question. They would be on him in moments if he ran. Would run right over him. Might not even know they'd done it. Just *whump*! Kid goo.

So he stood still, and when they seemed about to come over him, he shut his eyes. Whatever happened next, he was sure he didn't want to see it.

Everything suddenly became quiet and still.

Nobody ran over him. No clopping, thudding hooves making kid goo.

He opened one eye.

Then the other.

They had both stopped right in front of him and were holding their heads down to his level, smelling his hair. He reached out one hand and petted Jim on the nose. Soft, rubbery, and warm. Made him think of the word 'gentle'. Hot breath that rumbled and seemed to come out of a living cave. Damp warm air. He petted Blackie, touched his nose, the same thing. Like two enormously giant puppies, he thought. Just really big puppies.

Two tons of puppies.

Very slowly he reached up and put the lead rope loop around Blackie's neck behind his ears. Then he backed up a step and they both raised their heads and he turned and started to walk and they followed. He was hanging on to the end of the lead rope and they kept pace carefully so they wouldn't catch up or overrun him and hurt him. Like they'd been doing it all their lives.

They marched to the barn as perfect, as blue perfect (which was a way Sig had of saying something was going . . . exactly . . . right) as it could be. At the barn he stopped, they lowered their heads, he took the lead rope off Blackie's neck – and was brave enough to rub one of his ears in a kind of pet – and they went into the barn and moved on their own to a double stall at the east end, near the door.

Sig was waiting for them there and he put sweet feed in each of their licked-out boxes, and while they were eating the feed, he harnessed them both.

It was one of those things – harnessing them – that

was so complicated the boy couldn't quite follow along. First a big collar around their necks, then from the collar two thick leather straps that came back past their legs on each horse ending in chains about two feet long. Then a lot of smaller straps over their backs to hold the heavy load-pulling straps in place, then bridles with bits in their mouths, coming back with long leather lines – called reins – that the boy found later Sig would hold and use to turn or stop the horses.

He backed them out of the stall and, walking between their heads, went out the barn door and moved across the barnyard to where the boy had seen some farm machinery sitting. Most of it seemed old and had some rust on it, and he had thought it was mainly junk.

Wrong again.

One of the pieces of machinery had two wheels with a cupped seat over the middle and metal extensions hanging down with spade bits on the end of each of them. There was also a long shaft of wood jutting out of the front with a crosspiece near the machine. Sig swung the horses around, one of them – Blackie – stepping over the shaft (the boy found later this was called the 'tongue') so that one horse stood on either side of it.

All the time he had been talking to the horses, giving them instructions. 'Over, Jim, back, Blackie, back, back . . . hold there. Easy hold.' They worked to his voice and when they were in the right position and holding, he hooked the pulling chains to the crosspiece, then went to the front and pulled the end of the tongue until it was between the horses' necks and hooked it to both of them with a crosspiece attached at the bottom of the heavy collars.

With that finished, he turned to the boy. 'You ready to go?'

The boy was standing by the side of the horses and he looked at the rig. 'There's only one seat.'

Sig shook his head and, with one giant hand, reached down, scooped the boy up, and sat him on Blackie's shoulders. 'Hold on to those two little posts sticking out of the top of the collar. They're called the hames. You settle in there and hang on.'

At first, for a moment, he was about half scared. But the horses were so big and seemed so steady that when Sig got in the seat and picked up the reins and made a clucking sound with his tongue and they started to move, he didn't feel out of place at all.

They moved through the yard on the way to the cornfield and Edy saw them from the porch and waved and he let go long enough to wave back. Quick wave.

'Nice up there, isn't it?' she called. 'Like seeing from the top of a hill.'

At the cornfield, Sig lined the horses up so they each walked between two rows of corn, used a tall lever to lower the spade-shovel heads until they cut an inch or so down, skimming like knives, then he clucked once and never said another word.

The horses knew where to walk, how fast to walk, how to be careful not to hurt the standing corn – which stood about three feet high – and Sig and the boy were only along for the ride. The horses knew everything, and the cultivator – which the machine was called – just slid along, cutting at the roots, killing weeds.

The bloody things.

When the team reached the end of the row, they moved out a bit, turned in precisely the right way and exactly the right amount, and started back weeding two new rows on their own without a word from Sig.

By the end of that first row, the boy was completely accustomed to riding on Blackie's back – so wide it was like a living table – and nearly forgot he was on top of a horse.

Edy had been right. He was eight or nine feet above the ground and the view was noticeably different. He could see further, could see two deer nibbling corn at the far side of the field, could see fluffy white clouds scudding past the forest far to the south, could even see parts of the stream they had been on in the canvas canoe hunting mushrooms winding through the trees.

It was, in many ways, like a painting, a picture that would stay with him forever, a memory-picture. And in time, second row, third row, fourth row, the plodding horses, the warm sun, and the fresh smell of the corn combined to take him completely out of himself.

At first it wasn't that he slept, but that, with his eyes open and the comfort of the ride, he was there but not there. Finally, though, drifting in and out, he did fall asleep.

He must have shown he was losing control, or perhaps starting to lean, because he heard Sig stop the team in a soft voice and walk over to Blackie. Sig lifted the boy down and carried him back to the cultivator seat, climbing up and cradling the boy in his lap – still asleep – before making another soft sound and the team went back to work.

He was not sure how long he slept, or that it was really even sleep. He was very, completely, comfortable and felt . . . safe. Just safe. He thought then that he had never felt quite that way before, that he had always thought, felt, knew, believed, that there was some risk, some impending danger in his short life that kept him from relaxing into true, effortless safety.

But here – behind a team of horses, riding on a corn cultivator, sitting in a man's lap – he knew complete safety. Even the smells felt right, felt safe. Sweat smell coming back from the team, warm work-heat smell from Sig's dungarees, the soft feeling of his breath, chest in and out, up and down, wrapping around the boy, sheltering him.

He sank into it. Past sleep. Past awareness. Past anything. To safety, complete comfort and shelter, and he would not know for many years, for perhaps the rest of his life, a protection that was deeper than rest, a belonging that was a kind of love.

And he was out like that, wrapped in the shelter of Sig, until there came a time when he pulled the team to a stop and the boy opened his eyes to see that it was late day, evening, and they were back in the yard and Sig put the boy on the ground. He stood while Sig unharnessed the team and let them go behind the barn into the pasture.

The horses moved down the stream and drank while the two of them made their way to the house. Edy had milked and done the late chores but was still out in the barn, so Sig put wood in the stove and started a pan of meat and thin-sliced potatoes to frying.

The boy was still groggy from sleep, and he sat in a kitchen chair and thought of many things, thought that it was all the same and yet somehow different, that he was past just belonging, that he now fit, was part of how everything worked and would always be part of it.

And Edy came in from chores while Sig and the boy put dishes on the table and Sig dished the potatoes and meat and sliced thick bread for butter and honey and they ate and did dishes and the boy went up the stairs behind the stove.

Into *his* room, where he crawled into the blankets on his bed and went to sleep and didn't dream of anything except Rex chasing a butterfly like a big puppy. Which he didn't catch. But his tail kept wagging just the same.

And then no thing, nothing.

DIRT CANDY

The summer seemed to come in layers, one on another. He would learn one part – like chores or cultivating or the canoe or mushrooms or the bloody weeds – and something else would show up.

There came a day after chores and after they had breakfast that Edy looked at him across the table and said with a soft smile: 'You know what you are?'

'What?'

'You're our newest little potato.'

The boy had no idea what she meant, but she was smiling so he knew it was good, and if she wanted him to be their little potato, he would do that. So he nodded and said, 'All right. I'm your little potato, if that's a good thing.'

'Newest,' she corrected him. 'And not just the newest, but the best.'

'I don't know what you mean.'

She looked at Sig, who smiled and nodded. He reached across the table and tousled the boy's hair. 'It's like candy from dirt – you'll see this evening.'

When yard chores were finished and the barn cleaned, Sig had gone to the house while the boy was finishing up feeding the chickens. Sig and Edy came out of the house, and Sig had the big garden digging fork in his hand.

'Come on,' Edy said. 'To the garden.'

So he trotted across the yard and caught up with them, and they led him to a humped hill-row on the east side. It was obviously a potato row, but set apart from the other potato rows – he was about half proud there were no bloody weeds to see – and Sig dug under the first plant with the fork.

'We planted these early and covered them with straw so they wouldn't freeze.' Edy pointed at the fresh hole. 'Dig with your hands.'

The boy knelt and grabbed down into the soil. It was rich sandy loam and warm to the touch, and he felt something round and firm, and he pulled it up and there it was, a new small red potato.

'There's more.' Sig dug in again under the next plant with the fork and turned the dirt up. 'Keep digging.'

The boy did as he said and, in a short time, had found maybe five pounds of new red potatoes. Edy rubbed them clean with her hands and put them in a flour sack she had been carrying.

'Later this evening,' Sig said. 'Boiled and cut in pieces and eaten with salted butter – it's like God gave us dirt candy.'

'They're potatoes,' the boy said. 'We've eaten potatoes before.'

'Not like these.' Edy stood and brushed dirt from her knees. 'They don't last the winter like the big white potatoes, so you have to plant and eat them straight from the garden. You'll see.'

And she was right. She boiled them on the stove until they were so soft they would cut and mash with just a touch of the fork, and they ate them with butter and some brown gravy she made with a few of the mushrooms they had picked for extra flavour and they were . . . were like a candy. Right on the edge of sweet – the boy couldn't believe anything straight from the ground could taste that good.

He went to bed that night with a tight full belly and the fresh taste of buttery salt and new potatoes on his lips.

Along with a smile.

Made him proud to be called the newest best little potato.

In *his* bed.

GOOSE WAR

Sig had this to say about swearing when the boy was running barefoot in the pasture and stubbed his little toe on a rock and thought it was broken, and cut loose with a string of words he'd learned in the bars in Chicago: Swearing doesn't work if you use it too much, too often, too loud, and too stupid. Maybe a word now and then, if at all, and then it really counts.

So the boy asked him about the geese. He hadn't been talking about them regular because the bastards (thought, there, he used a swear, but maybe just this once) never let up and it would have been impossible to feed them into everything. Like he would start for

141

the barn and they would come after him, or he'd go to feed the chickens and they'd whump him and every . . . single . . . morning when he started for the outhouse, which was after breakfast to do his business, they would go for him.

And whump him.

And bite and pinch and use their wings to beat at him and every . . . single . . . morning Rex climbed into the bloody things (which was all right to say because he'd used it on the bloody weeds) and they would beat the peewadden out of him. (He didn't know what that word really meant but Edy used it all the time, like when the cats fought – 'They beat the peewadden out of each other' – so he thought it was all right.) They had a long talk and the three of them over dinner decided that's how it should be spelled: peewadden.

Which they beat out of Rex and pretty soon beat out of the boy and there came a morning, after he made a very close survival run to the outhouse and got clobbered on his way back to the porch, when Rex helped and afterward started walking with a bad limp.

He found Sig in the barn fixing harness – he had barely made it to the barn with the whole flock after him – and he stood inside the door, panting, on the edge of using all those not-good words from the Chicago bars, Rex standing next to him, panting just as hard, probably wishing he knew some not-good dog words as well.

'Why,' he said to Sig, gasping, 'do you have geese?'

Sig was sitting in the sunlight where it came in the front door on a three-legged milking stool. He cut off a string of lacing cord he had needled through a harness strap and laid it down across his knees, looked off into space, sighed, and said, 'You know, I don't quite know. Now and again, Edy will stuff a pillow with their feathers or cook with one or two of their eggs, and maybe once a year we'll have one for a celebration dinner. Like a Christmas goose, you know? So we keep them.'

'It's been weeks and weeks and they haven't backed off for a minute. They're going to kill me. Or Rex.'

He nodded and the boy thought, Well great, as long as it doesn't bother you I'll just go ahead and die. But Sig was thinking of what to say and when it was right in his brain, he said: 'When a thing comes at you to hurt you like that, you've got to go right at it and hit first. Make it hurt, and after a time, the thing won't come at you to hurt you so much.'

He stood and hung up the harness and beckoned the boy to follow him out the back door and down by the stream into a stand of green willow. He cut a piece about an inch and a half in diameter and maybe four feet long. He used his knife to peel the bark off in long strips, wiped the new wood dry with grass, and handed the boy the stick.

'What's this for?'

'It's your goose thumper. Next time they come for you, give a good growl, and head right into them. Swing left and right with the stick like you were Samson killing lions with an ass bone.'

'Really?' He'd never heard of anybody named Samson and wasn't at all sure exactly what an ass bone was or how you could kill lions by swinging left and right with it. But still. He'd been attacked by the geese week after week, so often it was nearly automatic for him to run from them. He was fear educated, fear trained. 'Really? Attack the geese. For sure really?'

Back in the barn, Sig stood by the door and pointed into the yard where the geese were permanently on patrol, always looking for something to attack. Usually the boy. 'I'll watch,' Sig said. 'If you get in trouble I'll come help. And you've got Rex, too.'

The boy came to the door and looked at them. The enemy. Then he looked up at Sig, who smiled, nodded again. 'Make noise when you go at them. A lot of noise.'

Well, the boy thought. Just that. Well.

Brandishing his new goose thumper, he moved into the yard and walked towards the geese. Rex had been standing with him and Sig and, sensing that things were going to get interesting, came out beside the boy.

As soon as the geese saw him, they started heading towards him. No delay. Wings spread, hissing, full-on attack mode, and for the better part of a second, his heart jumped into his throat and he came close to running. But Rex went for them and he couldn't let the dog go alone any more.

'Aaaaarrggghh!'

A kind of shriek-growl seemed to come from his stomach, or lower, and Sig said later he thought the boy was screaming. But it didn't matter. It was a loud noise, just a ripper of a sound, and he went for them.

Which didn't scare the birds at all. They kept coming, and in three jumps and a hiss and thumping wings, the air was filled with feathers and goose poop. He picked the first one – a mean grey gander – and hit him as blue perfect hard as he could. Fairly clocked him. And he went down – the boy thought he'd killed the goose and, frankly, didn't mind the thought at all – but he saw him a few minutes later get up, wobbling, and walk away from the fight.

Then the next one – Sig said later that he'd kept screaming – and the one after that and, from then on, he fairly swung left and right with the club until he had worked through the flock. Then he turned around and went back at them for a second pass. Climbed right into the middle of them – Rex and him – until, in a second, there wasn't anything around them but goose poop and feathers floating down. The geese were gone.

Didn't bother him again, the geese.

He carried the club for a couple of weeks to make sure. When he walked by them, they'd hiss bad goose words at him and flop a wing or two and one – had a crooked neck – would actually look away. But the war was done, and that night at dinner, Sig told Edy about the fight, said, 'The boy settled the goose problem,' and the boy didn't feel bad at how Sig seemed proud of what he had done.

So much for the geese.

The boy settled it.

One cool afternoon, he was weeding – he now did the same as Edy, pulling each weed by the roots, like extricating a disease, weeding with anger – and Sig came to the house. He had been down in the pasture near the stream and he called the boy to the porch. Edy was inside and she came to the door.

'They're running,' he said, as if that explained everything.

Edy nodded and showed a wide smile. 'Starting today?'

He nodded. 'We better get ready. They're starting late, so it might be a short run.'

'What's running?' Which the boy thought was an all right question, considering that he didn't have a single clue as to what he would see running in the pasture. Horses? Cows? And why were they running?

'Fish.' Sig looked back down at the stream as if visualizing something. 'The spawning fish run. Every spring after the ice goes out they run and lay their eggs upstream.'

'And we watch them?' The boy couldn't see what difference it made.

'We take them,' Edy said. 'We spear some of them and smoke them.'

So, he thought, that explained the little hut he had seen off to the side of the barnyard. When he'd asked about it, Sig had simply said, 'That's the smokehouse.' Which didn't help much but the boy knew Sig didn't like second questions when he had answered the first one. So he guessed they caught the fish or speared them and then lit them on fire in the little hut and smoked them.

No. No sense there. Hard to light a fish on fire. No more questions yet. He would learn as they went.

And what came, he found, were days and nights when they worked so hard it was possible to forget time, forget anything. Forget everything.

'Why don't you start the smoke fire?' Sig asked Edy. 'We'll get the chute ready.'

The boy followed him – it seemed that he spent most of his life following Sig; the boy who followed Sig – and they went down by the stream. Where it narrowed between the two banks, the boy saw a post that stuck up approximately in the middle of the stream, which was in line with a post buried in the soil of the near bank. He had seen all this before, and the roll of rusty netted wire fencing next to the bank post, so he'd assumed it was part of an old fence.

Wrong again.

As he watched, and then went to help, Sig pulled the canoe near to them from where it lay and slid it into the water with the nose still on the bank. Then he unrolled the rusty fence, wrapped the wires that pointed out of one end on the near post, gestured for the boy to help feed it out, and climbed into the canoe with the roll of wire. He paddled with one hand, unrolling the wire as he moved, out to the post in the stream, then pulled it tight along the bottom and attached it to the post in the stream. Set this way the netted fencing made an underwater barrier that would make anything swimming upstream have to go around it through the narrower opening at the end.

The fish, he thought. They'll have to swim through that narrow slot. He had naturally been looking for fish and hadn't seen any. The water seemed too dark, or else they were like the mushrooms and you had to learn to see them.

'Follow me,' Sig said after pulling the canoe back on the grass. 'Let's go see how Edy is doing.'

He was hurrying now and the boy had to nearly run to keep up. It was hard to believe the army hadn't taken Sig because of one of his legs being shorter or something. He never told the boy quite what it was; only that he had tried and they had turned him down because of his legs. The boy was at nearly a full lope just keeping pace with him. Seemed like that would be plenty good for the army.

At the little smoke hut, Edy had built a fire in a small pit about ten feet away. She covered the fire pit with a piece of sheet metal and put dirt over it. She had finished covering the sheet metal with dirt as they came up and the boy thought that seemed silly – to dig a hole and bury a fire.

Then he saw thick smoke coming out of the little hut and Edy saw his surprise. 'There's a stove pipe buried from the pit into the bottom of the hut – that way the smoke gets cooled. Cold smoke is better for the fish. Any meat, really. Sig likes smoked venison, too.'

Sig went to the granary and dragged an old table out

of the shed and put it near the fire. Then he went back in and came out with a wicked-looking fish spear – eight barbed tines that looked shiny, like they'd been filed sharp – on the end of a ten-foot wooden shaft.

'Get a bucket of water from the well,' he said to the boy. 'Slosh off the top of the table and then fill the bucket again and have it standing by the end of the table.' He thought a moment. 'Then get another bucket and hurry down to the canoe.'

'Bringing water?' He couldn't believe he'd need a bucket of water at the stream.

'No.' He was turned and gone, almost jogging with the spear, and called over his shoulder. 'Empty. Bring an empty bucket. Hurry.'

By the time the boy found a bucket in the barn and ran after him, he was already at the stream and had climbed into the front of the canoe with the spear, which put him leaning over the narrow part of the stream where the fish would have to swim around the netting to get through.

As the boy got there, Sig was intent, staring, before striking down suddenly into the dark water with the spear.

He came up with about a four-pound fish wriggling on the spear. He turned, wiggled the spear over the canoe and shook the fish off, looked to the boy. 'Bring the bucket into the canoe and put the fish in it. When the bucket is full, run it over to Edy and dump the fish out on the table, then run back down to me with the bucket.'

'How long . . . ?' He was going to ask how long it would take to fill the bucket but he had already turned, speared another fish, and shaken it loose inside the canoe while the boy was climbing into the end that was still on the bank. Both fish were still moving, flopping and bloody, from the spear holes.

The boy hesitated for a moment, then thought it couldn't be worse than worm goo or goose poop, and grabbed a fish by hooking his fingers through the gills, dropped it into the bucket, then the other one, and, by this time, Sig had already speared a third one, and a fourth one, which filled the bucket.

'Go,' he said without looking at the boy. 'Go now or the bucket will get too heavy. Don't waste any time.'

He took the four fish and clambered out of the canoe, ran to where Edy waited at the table – she was holding a long, curved knife – dumped the fish and turned back for Sig.

Where he already had six more fish.

The boy took four and ran them up.

Then back.

Four more.

And up and back and up and back, until somehow a whole day seemed to have passed and he was staggering with each bucket of fish and couldn't, honest to God, tell how many times he had run or whether or not he was heading up or down. Just fish and more fish, endless buckets of fish.

He didn't even count the buckets. Had no idea how many fish.

Way past tired.

Like his back and legs belonged to somebody else, somebody who hated him.

Flat numb.

Just numb.

Until at last Sig turned, said, 'That's all.'

He took the last four in the bucket, held the spear loosely in his left hand, bucket in the right, and loped – yes, the boy thought in horror, trying to keep up, he *loped* – back up the hill to where Edy stood at the table.

Oh, the boy thought. We're not done. He thought that maybe they were getting close to the end of this, this, whatever it was they were doing. Burning fish in cold smoke or something. But they were not done yet. Oh good. He staggered after Sig and found, to his shock and still more horror, that they were far from finished.

They hadn't really started yet.

Edy was at the table, wearing a rubber apron and flattening fish on the table. With one swipe, she cut the bellies open and scooped the guts out and into an old, rusty boiler next to her on the ground. Then, in the same motion, she split each fish down the middle so it splayed out flat, took handfuls of salt from a bag on the other – clean – end of the table, and rubbed it vigorously into the exposed meat.

Without a break Sig fell into place next to her with another knife, cutting and cleaning and dumping guts into the boiler, spreading and flattening and rubbing salt into meat.

Foolishly the boy thought: I don't see how I can really fit into this, until Sig motioned him to the boiler of guts. 'Get the straw fork from the barn and use it to put guts in the bucket we carried the fish in. When it's full, take it to the pigpen and dump it in the trough. Then come back and do it again. Oh, don't waste a lot of time or we'll get ahead of you – there'll be guts all over the ground.'

Silly of him not to see that – more work with the bucket. His job of work – gut buckets. Running with gut buckets. A mantra in his head: Running with gut buckets. Gutting with run buckets. Bucketing with gut runs. Guts. Running guts.

He would not have believed that there could be that much pure guts in fish. Running trip after trip with full buckets. Would never have believed that the pigs would eat them. Indeed, they appeared to love them and dived in as soon as the stuff slid, oozed, squelched into the trough. At first, he stared in a sick fascination, but then realized exactly what they were nosing into and tossing and eating, and after that, he looked away before . . . well, after that, he looked away when he emptied buckets.

Even later it would be difficult for him to remember anything in any kind of pattern. He ran with the guts, ran until his legs were past being on fire, past any feeling. And when the guts were gone, at last, all the fish that were spread open and salt-rubbed had to be hung in the little smoke hut on wires, so that the smoke went up and through them all. Sig stood in the door opening to the hut while he ran back and forth from the table and handed him salted fish, gulping and choking on the smoke that poured out of the open door, while the boy handed him the fish, two at a time, while Edy kept processing new ones for him to take to Sig and then run back to run, to run, to run . . .

Then more wood – from a pile of hardwood chippings that Sig had made with the axe – packed into the flame pit, covered with the metal sheet and more dirt, then hand more fish to Sig while Edy kept cutting and rubbing and he kept running and running and then . . .

Chores.

Cows to milk. Barn to clean. Eggs to pick. Chickens to feed and to keep out of the guts while the pigs ate them – the chickens were like feathered wolves after the guts, fighting the pigs.

Then more wood. Until it was end of day and the

sun was going down. Edy left them for a brief time and came back with thick sandwiches and a jar of milk for the boy. The sandwiches had a yellow filling that looked like BBs and tasted like fish. But everything tasted like fish, even the milk. And smelt, even the milk smelt like fish, and when he leaned down against the side of the smoke hut and tried to not sleep, he asked her what was in the sandwiches.

'Caviar,' she said.

'What's caviar?'

'Fish eggs. I took some out when I was cleaning the fish and fried them in butter. Good, aren't they?'

'Fish eggs?' He started to put the sandwich down. 'Like out of the guts?'

'And butter – only rich people eat like that. Caviar and butter. Good stuff. Aren't you going to eat it?'

And he did. He ate the sandwich because why? Because he was hungry, starved, and it tasted good. That's why.

'Wait until you have the stew.' She turned back for the house. 'It's one of Sig's favourites.'

'Stew?' He was sitting on the ground, leaning back against the side of the smoke hut. It was dark.

Everything was starting to spin and his eyes were closing while he fought to keep them open. 'What kind of stew?'

'Fish head. After they boil out I'll throw in some potatoes and we'll have fish-head stew tomorrow. Each head has thick cheeks that's the best meat on the fish. You suck the eyes out and eat them with cheek meat and new potatoes – Sig says it's blue perfect good.'

In truth he heard her but didn't hear her. He was dropping fast. And in seconds he was asleep. Sometime in the night somebody wrapped him in a blanket and let him sleep on next to the hut on the ground. He knew-felt somebody was close to him and he thought it was Sig because he had to stay there all night to tend the smoke fire. In the morning when the boy woke up, he was still there, sitting next to him, sleeping with his chin down and his arm over the boy's shoulders to keep him upright, sort of leaning against him, and he didn't mind.

Didn't mind at all.

And later that same day, in the evening after chores, they sat at the table for supper and he had fish-head stew with new potatoes and sucked the eyes out and ate the cheek meat and sopped up juice with chunks of new bread and butter and it was better than good.

He thought then – and still thought later as an old man – that it was right for him, everything was right for him right . . . then . . . blue perfect right, and he wouldn't have minded if it could go on and on and he could stay and not have the other part of his life. This part.

Shouldn't make plans.

Shouldn't ever make plans about how things should go.

Shouldn't.

About a week after they finished smoking fish and had eaten fish-head stew, he got to eat some smoked fish – brown and leathery and glistening with oil and salt – and he came to realize why they did it, why he helped to do it, smoked the fish. And he was playing hide from Rex in the cornfield – the corn was higher than him by this time – where he would run down a row, then step over three or four rows and call his name to see if the dog could find him.

And then Rex didn't come to look for the boy because he'd heard a car engine coming down the driveway and was chasing it, barking and growling as he bit at the tyres.

They almost never had cars drive in. As a matter of fact, it only happened once while he had been there, when a milk buyer came in a truck and wanted to buy any surplus milk they had.

But this was a different sound – a car, not a truck engine – and he made his way carefully through the corn to get back to the house. Truth was, he was a little shy. So he worked his way around to the front of the house to come in the front door quietly.

His mother was standing in the kitchen with a man he had seen in Chicago. Sig and Edy stood facing them, and the boy thought it strange nobody was sitting at the table and then he felt it. The tension in the room was so taut it seemed to hum.

He slid in the door.

His mother turned and saw him. 'Hi, sweetie, we're here to pick you up.'

He thought one word: But.

Just that. But.

'Uncle Casey is going to take us to Minneapolis and we're going to take the train out to California and then take a ship across the ocean to be with your father in a place called the Philippine Islands.'

But.

He couldn't leave . . .

But.

This is the place now, he thought.

His place, his place to be . . .

'Get your stuff,' she said. 'We have to get going.'

Sig shook his head. 'The boy fits here. He belongs to stay here.'

The man named Casey stepped forward. He was not the boy's uncle and would never be his uncle. He held up his hand, pointed to the door, and talked like he had a way to make it happen. 'We need to take the kid now.'

Sig grew bigger. Like that. Without moving he seemed to be bigger, to tower over the room. His voice was soft, but had sharp edges. 'You need to get from this house.' Still bigger, eyes hot. 'Now.'

And the man named Casey who was not his uncle moved, his eyes white with a new look, fear. Took a step back and the boy thought if Sig lights up on him, Sig will kill him. Just break him. And that didn't sound so bad, thinking on it.

But Edy stepped forward. Soft voice, woman's voice. 'No, Sig. Not now, Sig. He has to go with his mother, Sig.' Repeating his name like a soft song. 'We have to let him go now, Sig.'

Sig turned and looked at her and something settled in him, in his eyes and his body, and he settled, just that, settled. He still looked bigger, but settled, as if he were a dog and Edy was petting him, soothing him.

The man named Casey who was not his uncle went back out to his car and the boy smiled when he heard the geese go after him and then his mother went up the stairs and brought down his clothing and box and took his hand and pulled him out to the car and all the time Sig stood there next to Edy. They both came outside and stood watching.

And Casey who was not his uncle turned the car around and drove out of the yard, with Rex running alongside barking and biting at the tyres, and the boy watched out of the back window until they were out of sight, crying some, crying some, but nobody saw.

Just crying for himself. Just alone.

And all he thought was but . . .

But.

Part III

THE SHIP

THE POX

The train ride wasn't so bad.

He still missed Edy and Sig and thought of them almost every day and almost all the time with almost every breath and he had been on many trains by now and could not be surprised by them.

But this train went across the whole land and moved faster, and while there were still some wounded men riding to get home, this train was made for travelling faster and kept moving and you could sleep on it.

Plus they gave him his own bunk with a small window so he could look out from a bed that pulled down from the ceiling and see the country go by.

Something like camping only not really but made him sometimes not think only of Edy and Sig and the farm. As they moved west, he saw wide-open country and twice actually saw cowboys on horses.

So, not so bad.

And there was a dining car where they fed you clean meals with shiny silver and white tablecloths with small warm muffins that broke into three little parts that you could eat with a little square pat of butter that had a picture of a flower pressed into it and he thought Edy would love them.

All good.

And there was a club car that kept his mother busy drinking and talking to men who bought her drinks and bought him Coke in a clear glass with ice making the side of the glass drip with rivulets of cold water. It was clear that the men wanted him to leave after they bought him Cokes so they could talk to his mother and he didn't have to stand on a table and sing and he would move off and be ignored, which turned him loose and left him pretty much the run of the train.

And there was more to see and do as they rolled across the country with mountains and rivers and a giant lake that made it seem like the train was moving on top of the water when he could see ahead as it curved so that he stopped crying from memory thinking of Edy and Sig and only choked up a bit if he remembered things too clearly. Like the time with the geese when he won or when they smoked fish and he fell asleep against Sig's shoulder. He wondered about them, and about his grandmother, but already his life was full of abrupt and unexplained silences and departures. He knew you didn't ask.

And then it was San Francisco.

They arrived at night in thick fog and though they were to take a ship across the ocean to the Philippine Islands the ship wasn't quite ready to board so his mother found a very low-rent hotel on the edge of something called China Town, over a market that smelt of burned grease.

The people were kind enough, but he became ill, vomiting he thought from the smell of the grease, but then he developed pus-running sores all over his body and was told he had chicken pox.

In what a nurse who examined him called a full bloom. Like it was some kind of stupid flower. And his mother became cross with him as though he had contracted the pox on purpose just to ruin her trip on what she called 'the luxury liner.' Her anger grew more pronounced when she was told by authorities that the boy could not leave for a foreign country until he was over the chicken pox. Which they said would infect whole populations and possibly kill millions and it might take two weeks to a month for him to get completely clear of the disease.

And the ship was due to leave in a week.

So.

There it was – they would be stuck for maybe a month smelling burned grease.

But his mother talked to somebody who talked to somebody else and she met the captain of the ship in a bar not far from the hotel where she left the boy in the room, and the people who had been very kind to him spent a lot of time ignoring him for fear they would get the disease he had all over his body. Their fear grew so that while they actually fed him twice a day – his mother was nearly always gone – they would come to his room and leave a steaming bowl of sticky white rice often covered with some kind of greasy meat or vegetables and two little wooden sticks to eat with at the base of his door and knock and leave. The sticks he found were chopsticks and he couldn't come to grips with them except to scoop food off the lip of the bowl into his mouth. He thought they were overreacting to his sickness, but he admitted even to himself when he looked in a cracked mirror over a washstand that he was flat ugly. Like he was a walking sore with running pustules, and he thought if he had to do this for a month he would go right out of his little mind, as Sig would have said.

But there came a time in five or six days in the middle of a really dark night with thick fog when in the gloomy hotel room his mother and a man leaned over his bed and awakened him with gentle nudges.

'Just be very still,' his mother whispered. 'Mr Rigs is going to wrap you up and carry you.'

Not a blanket nor really a rug. A coarse tarp that smelt – as the man also smelt – of oil and grease and something else. Something new to him. Thick smell of new water. Salt water. And something of fish as well. Spoiled fish and salt water.

'Where—' he started to ask, but his mother cut him

off, pulled the end of the tarp over his head so he couldn't see.

'We're going to the ship,' she said.

'But didn't they say we couldn't leave until . . .'

'Mr Rigs is the captain of the ship and he said it would be all right. Now be still and be *quiet.*'

And they did this to him in that dark night. They put him in the back seat of a car sideways lying down, still covered with the tarp so he couldn't see where they were going, and in a time the car stopped and Rigs pulled him out and carried him like a floppy tube of rug or supplies over his shoulder. The smells grew stronger then – of salt water and grease – and there was sound, a low rumbling of motors somewhere near. Then up a sloping walkway where he could feel a new movement even through the body and right shoulder of Rigs and the rumbling grew louder, much louder and all around him. Then down steep stairs and clumping down an alleyway where he hit his head in sliding bumps along the side, another short turn, pause, and Rigs put him down on his feet and unwrapped the tarp.

His eyes were immediately attacked by white light so bright it seemed to come into his vision like needles. Blank, explosive white light and he closed them, opened them, closed them again and finally his vision settled down and he could see where he was – which made no sense at all.

Some small, white-painted steel cell with two bunks on the side wall and a toilet and small sink on the end of the cell welded to the wall. One light, one impossibly bright light, hung from the ceiling, and because everything – walls, ceiling, bunks – was painted in flat white, it made the light seem even still brighter and made him think of an indoor sun.

There was no opening to the outside world that he could see and he didn't have the faintest concept of where he might be. He was going to ask when Rigs pointed to the bottom bunk and said: 'This is where you'll live for a while.'

'But where are we?'

His mother was standing next to Rigs and she said, 'We're on the ship. The captain has let us come aboard in spite of some silly rules but you'll have to stay in here until . . .'

'Until what?'

'Until I say it's all right to come out,' Rigs said with

authority in his voice. Now that the boy could see him he found that in some way he matched the smell of him. Grease and salt and some fish smell and he looked like he had been put together somehow with used parts. Stooped but strong and in the manner of his odour, coarse, but entirely accustomed to having his orders instantly obeyed.

Rigs turned then and left the small cabin, and the boy found his mother standing by the entry with a small man. He had jet-black hair, cut very short on the sides, longer on top, and wore a crisp white naval uniform. The boy was going to ask his mother what had become a list of mental questions, but she had an odd look in her eyes and a green cast to her skin and looked like she was going to vomit, and she turned and hurried off with Rigs.

'She is seasick,' the small man said, shaking his head and making a clucking sound. 'We are still at the dock and just the harbour swell makes her sick. It sometimes happens to people who aren't used to being aboard a ship where they never get over being seasick.'

'Who are you?' the boy asked openly and then remembered being with Sig and how sometimes it was easier to learn when you didn't ask questions and kept your mouth shut but it was out there before he could stop it.

'I'm Ruben,' the man said, smiling. 'Take off your shirt, please.'

'What?'

'Take off your shirt and trousers. I must see your sores and clean the scabs away.' And the boy saw now that Ruben had a box of cotton swabs and a bottle of what turned out to be alcohol and the boy finally did as he was told and Ruben began dabbing at his poxes.

It hurt some – hot little stings when the alcohol-soaked cotton first came in contact – but the boy thought of fighting the geese and stood for it and took the time to question Ruben.

He learned many things.

First, Ruben was a young man from the Philippine Islands, a Filipino, and had joined the United States Navy right after the start of the Second World War. His job on the ship was to be a steward, a helper, and that included odds and ends of medical work he had to do from time to time on the crew and/or passengers. He was very kind to the boy and seemed to have a soft smile to match his soft voice whenever he saw the boy, which was every day for the time the boy was confined in the small cell.

And it was a cell. The boat was most decidedly *not* a seagoing luxury liner as his mother thought. It was right on the edge of being an old crate – one of the so-called liberty ships made rapidly by the Kaiser Shipyards during the war – and had spent most of its life ferrying troops and equipment from island to island. It was mostly in usable shape but had some rough edges. 'She is tired,' Ruben told him. 'The ship is tired. She needs some rest.' The so-called room that the boy was kept in had been the cell – called the 'brig' – for men who broke the law and had to be confined.

One of the first times he used the toilet in his cabin the boy flushed with the small lever on the wall and suddenly felt the ship move. Thinking he had done something wrong, the boy ran back to his bunk, but the movement did not stop, and it felt like they were first going sideways, then backwards, then forwards, all at once.

The room was so bright that the boy didn't think he could ever close his eyes, but something from the rhythm of the engines and the motion of the ship relaxed him completely and he slept easily.

Although time was hard to keep in control – he could see no sun nor darkness and had no way to tell day or night – he would find later he had been kept there for ten days. He measured the days by counting meals, which Ruben brought him twice a day, and by Ruben taking the time each day to dab away his scabs.

His mother came down twice to see him in those ten days but was almost completely destroyed by her motion sickness, especially after they left San Francisco and moved (and 'moved' was the right word) into the open Pacific Ocean. The ship rode gentle swells that came from the rear and helped slide it gracefully across the surface of the sea, and the boy found the motion to be enjoyable and so restful he slept during the sleep periods like he'd been hit with a soft hammer. But the same motion left his mother deathly ill. Every day Ruben updated him with reports about her. 'She keeps near a bucket all the time,' Ruben told him. 'She is a pretty woman but has to be close to a bucket.' The boy could tell from Ruben's expression that he found this amusing although he was trying not to show it.

In many ways the boy did not mind the absence of his mother. The ship and the throbbing of its engine that came through the steel in the hull and the walls surrounded him and became a kind of music, a lullaby when he wanted to sleep, an assurance when he was awake and reading comic books.

Or eating candy.

There were many men on the ship and they all wanted to meet his mother, to know his mother, and they thought he could help them if they impressed him. They could not come to see him in what he came to know and understand as his medical confinement, but they quickly found out that Ruben saw the boy every day and they virtually accosted him with comic books and candy to give to the boy along with notes they hoped he would show his mother, but in the way of things the ship itself – herself? – had become his parent.

A mother ship?

Sometimes alone in his bunk he would hang on the edge of sleep and would push to the side so the top bunk would make a shadow from the overhanging light – which was never out – and press his hand flat against the steel of the wall and feel, *know*, the engine throbbing as if it were a warm, beating heart, that would take him into sleep.

Days passed, folded, and when Ruben had time he would tell the boy about his home in the Philippine Islands, in the great city of Manila, and weave stories – always happy stories – of his time there and the people. The boy went from initially knowing nothing to thirsting after more knowledge. From the start, he had no concept of what the Pacific Ocean was – Ruben said it was the biggest thing on the whole planet – and going to the Philippines was in the nature of a fairy tale. He wanted once to know if there were magical genies there to answer three wishes, which he had seen in a comic book, and monsters. In the end, it turned out there were no genies to answer three wishes but there were, or had been, monsters, and he would see and live in what they had destroyed and left partially standing.

He had much more to ask about the Philippines but Ruben had many other duties aboard the ship – one of them was taking care of and tending to the boy's mother. Emptying the bucket and bringing damp cloths for her forehead and forcing her to drink all she could to keep her from becoming critically dehydrated because she couldn't stop vomiting.

Twice in the boy's confined time Ruben came into

the cell looking pushed, harried, and said: 'We must clean the cabin now. Captain Rigs will inspect it.' And he worked with and drove the boy to make the bed and stack comic books neatly on the foot of the bed and they used damp rags he had brought to wipe down all the surfaces in the room. When he was done, he stood at attention near the door, made the boy stand the same as Rigs came in, looked briefly around the cell, rubbed a white-gloved hand on a surface near the bunk and looked at the dust on his finger, shook his head, and left.

The boy wanted to ask him how long he had to stay in the cell, wanted to ask him how far they had come and when would they get to Manila, but never got a word out. He turned to Ruben and said 'Are we in trouble because his finger got dirty?'

Ruben shook his head. 'He always finds something. He has to find something or he's not the captain, right?'

SHARKS

The routine remained the same until the boy had in the end accepted that it would probably go on forever. Steel tray of food in the morning – powdered eggs, creamed corn, and white bread – followed by, if there was time and he didn't mind, a conversation with Ruben while he used the alcohol-cotton swabs to dab at his sores, and then a day reading comic books and thinking about what Ruben had told him of the Philippine Islands. Until later in the day when he got another steel tray of food – very often fried liver, instant dry mashed potatoes, two more slices of white bread without butter, some absolutely god-awful desiccated string beans mixed with watery kidney beans, and a candy bar for dessert from the men who wanted to meet his mother. Twice Ruben brought him a can of pork patties cold in lard and a second can – the cans were coloured olive-drab – with something called a pound cake for snacks. He was so fat-starved he actually enjoyed the pork and lard cold, and the pound cake tasted truly good. Sweet. And oddly fresh considering that both these cans were from leftover army rations.

The boy had accepted that the situation would last forever, or for however long it took to get to Manila, and on the tenth or eleventh day – he could not be sure of the time – Ruben came rushing into the cell and said: 'Come quick. A plane is coming down.'

Which made no sense at all and the boy asked, 'What plane?'

Ruben ignored the question. 'Come quick. I must help. Please follow and find your mother so she can look after you.'

The boy did not need a second invitation and he ran out after Ruben, wearing shorts and an old T-shirt. They virtually loped through what seemed like endless white steel tunnels and up a metal ladder-staircase and through a side door until they were suddenly out in the open on the side deck of the ship.

Initially it was so bright and blinding that it was almost as bad as when he was first introduced to the cell. He closed his eyes, wiped the sudden light-tears away, opened them, closed again, and finally got them to stay open.

All he saw was blue.

He had never seen the ocean before, had no real idea of what it would be like, and all he saw, all he could think, was the word 'blue'. It was as if he and Ruben and the ship, his whole world, was at the bottom of a startling bright blue bowl that reached into the sky.

Blue.

And calm. Like it had been laid down with a ruler. The ship had stopped and the boy saw that they were lowering a large lifeboat down the side on ropes until it floated free. There were men in the lifeboat and they started an engine in the middle of the boat and other men were unfolding a portable staircase that went down the outside of the ship. Just as the boy looked towards the bow and saw his mother standing, leaning weakly against the side of the main cabin, he heard the sound of plane engines.

The plane passed over the ship quite closely – he could see rivets and other markings plainly – and made two gently dropping circles. It had four engines and numbers on the wings and American symbols – a circle with a star in the middle – painted on the bottom of the wings. Other than that it was shiny aluminium and looked clean. He would find later – would, in fact, see many of them in the Philippines – that they were military transport planes called C-54s. But for now all he could think was that it looked huge and that the engines, which he at first heard but did not really listen to, were running ragged and one of them was leaving a thin trail of yellow-black smoke.

He was and remained alone. His mother was barely able to stand where she was and Ruben went off to help other men get ready to . . .

What? he thought. Is the plane really going to land out here in the water?

And then?

Get the passengers out of the plane? Is that what they're after? Why they put the lifeboat down?

Won't the plane sink?

After that, nothing that happened looked or felt sensible to the boy.

The plane made one more circle back and over the ship, then the engines sounded lower, more choppy, and the plane glided down so gently and peacefully that the boy thought: He's going to do it. He's going to land smoothly right on the water. Like there's a run-way.

But no.

The ocean looked completely flat, calm. But there was a little swell and when the plane at last touched down – it seemed to hang in the air and take forever – it did not hit evenly. The end of the right wing clipped the water first, then grabbed deeply and seemed to slam-jerk the plane around, to the right, but the energy was too great and the plane broke, separated behind the wings and turned into two pieces and the rear portion started to sink immediately.

It was then the boy saw that the plane had been filled with people – mostly women and children – and they seemed to explode out in a shower of tumbling figures into the water around the sinking plane.

The lifeboat and men were headed for it as fast as

they could but they were still a good distance away and seemed to be moving slowly.

So slowly.

The plane had landed so that it was about a quarter of a mile from the ship, close enough so the boy could see that the people in the water were wearing bright yellow inflatable life vests and floating upright. The front of the plane was sinking but much more slowly and some of the people and kids were trying to get back on the wings, which were just at or slightly beneath the surface.

The boy had been on the far side of the ship, away from the side where the plane had landed, but he made his way across the ship through an opening until he was at the rail leaning out from the side. From this position he could see a little better and hear as well and the people were yelling and trying to help each other.

As he watched, he saw, or really sensed, motion in the water near the ship and he looked to see large grey shapes leaving the stern and streaking in the direction of the plane and within what seemed like only moments the people in the water began screaming and thrashing at the surface and some of them jerked and went under, came up and were jerked under again.

'Sharks.' A soldier standing at the rail near the boy had been watching. 'The devils follow the ship looking for rubbish and they're going after the women and kids . . .'

From that moment on, it became something close to a nightmare but the boy could not take his eyes away. He did not know anything about sharks, or how many there were, but even as the lifeboat reached the sinking plane and the men in the boat started pulling the people out of the water, he could see that the sharks were not giving up. They hit the legs and feet of the women and kids while the men pulled at their tops to get them clear. It seemed like everybody was screaming – shrill, ripping screams as they got hit – and even at this distance he could see the red froth of blood in the water near the boat.

In a time that seemed to be forever, at last, the men had saved everyone who had not been pulled under and came back to the ship and they started lifting and carrying the women and kids from the lifeboat on the side of the ship.

187

The boarding stair-ladder was on the side of the boat away from the plane – which had now disappeared completely as it went down – and the boy ran back across the ship to the top of the stair in time to see the first of the survivors being carried aboard.

There was an unbelievable amount of blood. It had mixed with seawater and covered the sailors carrying the wounded, dripped onto the deck, covered the wounded themselves, some women, some children, and many of them had been hit by the sharks, had tears and rips in their sides and legs and arms. The boy saw Ruben there, meeting them, trying to give them first aid as the sailors carried them inside the top cabin of the ship.

And more than that he was stunned to see that his mother had apparently fought off the seasickness and had rolled up her sleeves and was helping Ruben working with the injured, wrapping bandages tightly over the wounds trying to stop the bleeding.

He had never thought of her this way and he felt proud that she could do this . . . this help with these really awfully, horribly wounded people. He had himself leaned over the side, or tried to lean over the side, and vomited when he saw one boy whose stomach was ripped open. And here she was, like she'd been doing this all her life, following Ruben into the large central cabin where they laid people out on the deck and chairs, going from one to the next, talking softly. Softly. And while he watched he saw her push some hair out of a woman's face and say something soft to the woman, and the boy was certain the woman died at that very instant with her upper chest torn open so he could see . . . so he could see.

It was, finally, too much.

He made his way out onto the deck, trying to not see, did not want to see such a thing ever again, and found sailors hosing blood-water off the deck and made his way to the stern. The ship had started moving again and he looked down and saw the grey shapes in the water, following the ship, and he tried not to look at them but he did. He did look.

And then he sat quietly on the deck and leaned back against the sun-warmed steel of the mast housing and stared out at the ocean and tried not to think on all that he had seen, and heard, and smelt. Hot, thick stink of blood and blood-screams and salt water. The sea. The blue. The giant blue and the shiny aeroplane and the sharks. Grey death.

New thoughts. Some quick, new, good thoughts before his brain was filled with the horror . . .

Edy and Sig. Wonder what they were doing and how could he have been there a few weeks ago, been in that wonderful place, that place where everything was beautiful and made sense and be here now?

Here.

How could that be?

With people torn to shreds and blood and guts and screams and his mother, his mother, his mother . . .

And he curled up on the warm deck and closed his eyes and slept.

MANILA

In some strange manner he could not find anything wrong with Manila. It had been nearly destroyed, gutted – often literally – by the Japanese army during the occupation. Blown apart, torn to pieces, burned . . .

And yet.

And yet he came to love it.

The ship had stopped briefly in Honolulu and left the survivors from the plane wreck, where – God help them – they would have to get back on yet another plane and return over the same ocean to the United States.

And then the ship stopped at some other islands to drop off small bits of military supplies, but the boy hardly noticed they had stopped.

After the plane crash he only returned to the cell to sleep. And indeed, did not always do that but slept in various places on the deck and became a wild thing, sleeping when he felt like it, eating when he felt hungry. Ruben had introduced him to the galley on the ship and the cook, who was also Filipino. He was a big man and liked the boy and would give him a roll or a sandwich or a bowl of rice with a can of sardines dumped on top whenever he felt like eating.

The large central cargo hold was essentially sealed off with bolted hatches but he had the run of the rest of the ship, and in the remaining two weeks of the trip there wasn't really a part that he didn't see, although – except for a quick look – he didn't spend any real time on the bridge. Captain Rigs was there most of the time and didn't seem to want to spend a great deal of effort caring about or knowing the boy.

But the rest of the ship was like a playground to him, filled with nooks and crannies and hidden places.

His mother had returned to her seasickness as soon as she stopped helping with the plane crash survivors and the boy had stockpiled a good supply of comic books and candy, although any chocolate bars had to be eaten soon as they always melted in the heat. But the peanut bars seemed to last better and he found a cubby near the stern where he would sit and eat candy and read comics.

He did not spend any time looking over the stern. The sharks followed in a weaving pattern and when he did look he could not see them without thinking of the grey streaks heading for the people in the water.

So no looking back.

But the sea seemed to take him. He loved the colour of it, the way it rose in front of him, pulling at him, beckoning, and he was never bored with it. He could sit and watch it, wondering at the immensity of it, and in fact was doing just that on an early morning when they reached Manila.

He had been in the galley before dawn and the cook gave him some toast with canned strawberry jam on it and he went outside on the deck to sit and eat it when he looked up and saw there was a looming dark landmass to the side. The air had a heady smell, a rich almost green tang, a mix of plants and animals and mustiness and heat and moisture. He had heard nothing from anybody that they were even close to someplace, and now the ship slowed to a crawl and turned in the new dawn light and worked its way towards a huge pier and he could see an enormous city behind the pier.

As the sun rose the light grew and he could see more and saw that there were swarms of people, thousands of them who seemed to be rushing somewhere and made him think of an anthill on Sig and Edy's farm when Sig kicked the top and the ants came boiling out.

Just everywhere. And they seemed to be moving towards the ship. The boy ran to the side to get closer, to see more, and he saw a soldier standing on the pier with one hand on his hip casually holding a Thompson submachine gun butt-propped on his other hip with his right hand on the pistol grip and index finger across the face of the trigger guard. When he saw the boy, the barrel of the submachine gun slid slowly to the side until it was aimed directly at the boy's face. He would find later that wherever this man looked, the barrel of the gun followed, centred, held.

The boy thought at first it might be his father but when he looked closer he could see that the man in no way resembled the tinted picture he had seen. Thinner face. All angles. And from what he could see, his eyes looked . . . looked cold. The boy started to turn to go for his mother but she appeared suddenly and grabbed him by the arm and took him below where a small door was opened onto a gangway the sailors had placed across to the pier.

'Come on!' She hissed the words. 'Let's get off this tub onto some dry land.'

Without giving him a chance to say goodbye to Ruben, she dragged him down the ramp of the gangway until they hit the pier and then she let him go and began looking frantically up the pier through the milling crowds of people.

The man with the machine gun came forward. Eyes and gun barrel looked up and down his mother, then down to the boy. The barrel of the machine gun looked like a cave.

'I'm Sergeant Cramer,' the soldier said. 'Your husband has duty and couldn't get away. I'm to pick you up and take you to your quarters.'

Voice cold, flat. Like it came from night somehow. Not from him, exactly, nor out of him but around him. 'I'm to pick you up . . .' Wasn't a request but an order and when he finished he turned and said something fast and hard to a Filipino man behind him in a language the boy couldn't understand, then back to his mother, gun barrel on her face. 'He'll get your baggage.'

'How will he know . . .'

'He'll know. Come this way. I have a jeep waiting.'

And he turned and was gone. His mother grabbed the boy by the arm again and followed. Cramer moved so fast they nearly had to run to keep up until at last they threaded their way through people to the head of the pier and the boy saw an olive-drab jeep sitting there. He climbed into the back seat and his mother took the front passenger seat and the Filipino man brought two suitcases and stacked them in the rear seat next to the boy. The man did not try to get in the jeep but turned and seemed to disappear in the crowd and Cramer started the jeep and they took off.

Almost literally.

Cramer seemed to have only one speed – wide-open, with nothing even resembling a seat belt – and the boy and his mother were nearly thrown from the vehicle.

'Shell craters in the road,' Cramer said. 'Hang on. It's better to get over them fast or we'll sink in too far . . .'

They seemed to go right through the middle of the city and in the end Cramer had to slow the jeep to get through the crowds of people, so the boy could see some of what they passed.

It looked in many ways like a wasteland. Bombs and artillery and mortars had blown everything apart so that he didn't see any undamaged standing buildings. One ancient ornate Spanish building that the boy thought might have been a church had an enormous round hole blown – it must have been forty feet across – through the middle so you could see completely through the whole building.

It was like somebody insane had tried to hurt an entire city.

And had succeeded. The damage was there, the hurt.

But there was another side the boy saw. As they drove through the crowds it seemed that most of the men he saw were dressed in shorts and loose white or khaki shirts. The women wore either tight skirts or loose wraparound skirts and blouses. Although some of them shouted or made rude gestures at Cramer for his dangerous driving, almost everybody they passed seemed to wave to the boy and smile. Seemed to have joy. Joy amongst the wreckage of their city.

And the joy made him think suddenly of Edy when he first arrived at their farm and she came to meet him in the driveway when he was faced – he thought – with the threat of the geese. The happiness he felt then when he recognized her.

And here. It was the same here. The feeling here was one of invitation, of cheer, of being recognized, known, and he thought immediately that he belonged.

That it was for him, of him. He could not know anything of the city except what Ruben had told him now and then on the ship. But he had been hurt, frightened, hurt in some ways the way this city had been hurt, and now they smiled. Waved. Called to him. Greeted him.

As if he belonged.

Belonged to Manila.

He knew nothing but one thing.

One thing was certain.

He wanted to see more of this place, know more of the city and how the people could have such Edy-like joy.

He must know more of Manila.

STREET RAT

But first . . .

It seemed that his whole life to date was a series of those 'but firsts'.

Before he did this, he had to do that. Before he came across the ocean, somehow he had to go through chicken pox. Before he saw Edy and Sig, he had to sing in bars in Chicago and help his mother meet men who were not his uncle.

And now first, he had to meet his father.

Which proved to be if not exactly pointless at best boring.

Cramer drove through a military gate and took them to their new house, which was all screens, no windows, and – the only thing really interesting – a ceiling covered with small lizards that horrified his mother and she was going to sweep and kill every last one of them until a servant named Maria said they were not to be killed because they were good luck and ate mosquitoes. Apparently the house came with with two servants – Maria and a young man named Rom. His father called them his house girl and house boy, which made no sense to the boy as Maria and Rom were both grown-ups, not children. Maria had long black hair that hung down her back and a small, slight body that made her seem almost tiny though she was nearly as tall as Rom. She had huge brown eyes and always wore flowered wraparound skirts and white shirts that looked both wrinkled and very clean. The boy learned she had a child, who she brought to work sometimes, and Rom had lived in the centre of the city of Manila in a ramshackle hut made of wooden ammunition boxes and roofing tin.

Along with lizards and servants the house came with rattan furniture, a small kitchen, and a mat covered with Japanese letters on the floor. The Japanese soldiers had taken all the houses when they occupied the Philippine Islands, along with everything else.

The boy was sitting on a rattan couch reading a comic book – somehow his stash of comic books had come with the suitcases – when his father came in.

He was tall and thinner than in the picture the boy remembered and wearing a uniform so starched it looked like it would hold him up.

He glanced at the boy and the boy thought: Captain Rigs.

Just a mere glance. No touching. No hugging. Nothing even remotely close. Not even a smile. The boy could have been – and this would hold true for the father's whole life – somebody else's child. The father looked once, turned away, and ordered – not asked, but ordered – Maria to bring him a drink.

And the mother had a drink.

And that was it. Welcome home, the boy thought.

And then more drinks.

And finally they were drunk and fighting, screaming at each other about other men and other women, his mother throwing dishes and ashtrays at his father, and the boy curled into his bunk in the alcove that was supposed to be his room and tried to not listen, not hear, not know. And would not and could not even imagine that they would be here for just under three years and every night that the boy was in the house – and in the end there would be many nights when he was not – they would be the same.

One drink.

Two drinks.

Then more.

Then fight.

Impossible to see, to do, to be this. First night screaming, drunken fights and then more and more . . .

No joy here.

Maria and Rom took pity on the boy when they saw how things were in the house. Rom told him that Maria had been hurt herself and horribly used by the Japanese but still she tried to help the boy all she could, making extra sticky rice for him to eat with a can of sardines she opened and put on the rice with a salty, special sauce.

Sardines. Oily, packed tightly in the small cans with a windup lid, smelling when he first opened the can like, well, canned sardines. Fins, guts and all.

Rom had a family in the city, with children – the boy never quite knew how many there were since the number always varied because Rom fed any street child that showed up at his door – but he always seemed to have time to help the boy. Rom had an old fat-tired Japanese military bicycle with a strong rack on the back that would hold the boy, and anytime the boy wanted to go somewhere, Rom would put him on the back straddling the rack and take off, his long thin arms roped with muscle steering them down one street after another.

Initially they mostly stayed within the boundaries of the housing compound where the boy lived, marked by tall barbed-wire fences with guard towers almost as if it was a prison. It was at the edge of a much larger military reservation, which stretched for miles. From an airstrip, planes were constantly taking off and landing – C-47s, C-54s, Mustang and Thunderbolt fighters – and the boy liked to be near the end of the strip to watch and listen to their thunder.

But when it became evident that the parents didn't seem to care very much what happened to the boy, Rom started taking him into the city to his shelter, which the boy found was built of ammunition-box wood and corrugated roofing tin, part of a block away from the ornate building with a hole blown through the middle.

Rom's wife had been killed by an explosion when the war fought through the city and it left him caring for his own children and – because he was the kindest person next to Edy and Sig the boy had ever seen – he kept a large pot of rice going for the street orphans. This he fortified with scraps and vegetables from mess halls he visited once a week and what seemed to be hundreds and hundreds of olive-drab-coloured cans of sardines. When the boy asked where the sardines came from, Rom shrugged, made a small smile, and said, simply, that he 'borrowed' them from friends and neighbours who worked for other Americans. The boy came to like, then love, sardines and sticky rice, which he ate off a piece of cardboard or newspaper and would enjoy the rest of his life.

At first the boy spent most of his time in the city with Rom, near him, sometimes helping with the rice. But as he became accustomed to being there he started heading off alone, exploring the ruins, feeling the noise, the smells, the raw life of the place.

As month fed to month it became, if not exactly a playground, a kind of home. Soon he found himself wearing shorts and a tired almost-white T-shirt and tennis shoes, squatting next to a ruined, blown-out building eating rice and sardines with his fingers.

Feeling a spark of joy.

Except.

Except he would find there were many Manilas.

There was the daytime Manila, where everybody smiled and waved and would reach out to tickle him when they walked by.

And there was the Manila of the night.

When he had been there a month or so, still before he actually went into the city with Rom, he began to hear the pounding of heavy machine guns at night. At first, he was not sure what they were – the sound was dense, sodden, like somebody rapidly hitting a flat board with a large hammer floating on water – they came in short bursts, eight, ten flat explosions and then a pause and another burst. When he asked Rom about them, about the sounds, Rom merely shrugged – his answer to many questions – and said something about the night people – these being guerilla soldiers who had lived in the forests and attacked the Japanese occupiers during the war – daring resistance fighters who were now battling against the new occupiers, the Americans.

'They want things to change,' Rom said.

'What things?' the boy asked.

'All things,' Rom said sadly.

The night people.

And there came a night, a long night when in the middle of the hard dark and his parents were passed out, he was awakened by the deep sound of the machine guns and decided to go outside and see what was happening. The dependent housing was close to the boundaries of the base, and when he got on the porch, he could see searchlights sweeping and hear the sound of guns but could not see much more.

Had to get a little closer.

And still closer.

Out onto the street and over one block and down another block and still another and then . . .

Then he could see.

The lights were sweeping the boundary fence and men were trying to climb the fence and the silver-white beam from the searchlight would catch them, pin them, and the machine guns would stutter-slam and tear them off the fence and down.

Blown apart and down. It was a distance away but the

boy could see the red streaks of the tracer bullets going through the men's bodies; he was told later that the tracers were only one of every five bullets, and the men were hit by all the bullets, not just the tracers, and torn into a red mist and turned into something that was not men.

Not men.

The night people.

Almost every night he heard the sounds of the guns. Sometimes further away, on some other part of the boundary where even if he went outside he wouldn't be able to see it.

But he didn't do that.

Didn't go outside to see it again.

Didn't want to see that again. Like the sharks in the red water. Not ever.

The next morning when Rom came to take him on the Japanese bicycle, they went past the place where the fighting had occurred and the bodies were still there and there were dozens, scores of colourful chickens working at them and the boy tapped Rom on the back:

'Chickens?'

Rom nodded without turning his head. 'From fighting roosters. There must be chickens to hatch roosters for cockfights. Some went wild, others went more wild, and soon there are wild chickens.'

'But why here?'

'Men who come at fence sometimes have rice balls in pockets. Chickens are after rice balls.'

'Aren't they afraid of the guns?'

'They are hungry and are after rice balls,' Rom repeated. 'And sometimes other soft parts . . .'

Had to ask. 'What do you mean, other soft parts?'

Rom shrugged. 'Eyes. Some other places left open by the bullets. But mostly rice balls and eyes.'

'Really?' He tried not to think of a chicken pecking the eyes out of a dead man but could not . . . quite . . . kill . . . the thought-picture. 'Truly?'

Another shrug. 'Night people.' As if that explained everything. 'They're night people. You are young and do not need to think about them . . .'

Night people.

To not think about.

But he did.

And he did not stay young long.

Manila was darkened at night because the Japanese had destroyed the power plants. The Americans had dragged a Japanese submarine to the pier to act as a source of electricity, but it only put out a limited amount of power and until the power plants could be rebuilt much of Manila was dark.

Candles.

Some lanterns here and there.

But dark.

With moving shadows and night people.

And after that, a part of him, a part of his spirit, was calloused and toughened. Like leather.

And he would not and could not be young again.

Ever.

Part IV

THIRTEEN

SAFE PLACES

Because it was safe there.

In the library.

Only three places safe. The library, moving through the alleys at night after hard dark and, best of all, the woods.

But in town, if you had to be in town, it was the library first. That was best. Alleys only if you had to move, and keep moving. They were second best. But the woods, feeling the forest fold in around you, closely behind you like a soft blanket layered over and around you – best of all. The woods were the best.

Not home. Never home. Not with Them there. Not

really a home; grubby apartment that he thought of as a dark, damp, wet ugly nest of . . . he didn't know what. Later in life, when he found himself remembering against his conscious will, when he couldn't keep the memories back in the dark place, he would think of the word 'vipers'. Dark, wet nest of slithering vipers. Drunk, mean: viper drunks so that even when they were passed out after the screaming and fighting, passed out like they were dead – never that lucky; that they really would or could be dead; never that lucky – even when they were passed out and down that far it wasn't truly safe.

What if they woke up? Caught you moving through the house silently walking on the balls of your feet, moving like a shadow in the dark, finding what food you could, taking money from their purse and trousers, woke up and caught you? Then what?

Not safe.

And now, now that he was thirteen, just thirteen, first-time thirteen, only time in his whole life when he would be thirteen, everything was different now, new sounding, and it had to be safe. Safer.

He was old enough now to run. To run away and

make it stick. He had run before. Run twice. Ran out into the great space west – no, West – ran out into the prairies, hitchhiking into the giant, wonderful, losing space of North Dakota, and found work on farms. Two, three dollars a day and not too many questions asked about why such a young boy would be alone. Told clean lies looking down at the ground and sniffling like he was lonely and going to cry, clean lies about being an orphan: mother killed in a car wreck, father in the war fighting the Germans. Clean lies, hopeful lies, no questions. Two, three dollars a day with slop food called stew full of chunks of soft-slippery meat that didn't smell like any meat he'd ever had, slop twice a day on a wooden bench from metal pie plates nailed down to the plank table with a galvanized roofing nail in the centre. A bent metal spoon and two pieces of dry bread and sandy water smelling of sulphur. Still all right. Better than back there – Back There – near home. Slept in a barn or equipment shed on gunny sacks until somebody, some neighbour, some busybody told somebody else who told somebody other than that and then a county sheriff.

Called a runaway. Like he was escaping jail.

Detained – not arrested, they said, but detained – and sent home with a church volunteer do-gooder. Big man with red cheeks who talked about how the boy should Work to Find Jesus in his Life and after three hours of driving in an old Dodge, he dropped the boy at his home where the boy knew Jesus never lived. Like putting a sheep back with wolves, dropping the boy where Jesus never lived. Or even visited. Maybe, the boy thought, Jesus might sometimes be in the library.

Where it was safe. Sure not safe at home. Never safe. Parents didn't know he was gone anyway and when they at last thought to punish him for running, for being a runaway – no, Runaway – he was already in the woods. Father said he was no good. Swore at him. Called him worthless. This from a man who got so drunk he pissed his trousers and didn't know it. Walked back from the liquor store with a bottle in a paper sack and wet legs and didn't even know it. Broad daylight, front of God and everybody, probably even Jesus, and didn't even know he was wet-legged.

But called the boy a worthless kid.

Sure.

Worthless kid who never pissed his trousers and

was smart enough to slip away before they knew he was gone and head for the woods.

Clean gone.

Safe.

Ran twice and the second time was nearly the same except that he hitchhiked still further west – West – and learned to drive a two-ton grain truck and a big M-model Farmall diesel tractor. Had to sit on an old Sears catalogue in the truck to see over the steering wheel and work the gear stick with both feet on the clutch and both hands on the top knob of the gears. Over left and back for low gear with a little grind, right and up for second, straight back for high, but he got her done, by God. That's what the farmer said: 'You got her done, by God.' And he did. Good compliment. Made him feel older. Not thirteen yet but made him feel older like he had more shoulders. Or thought they felt that way. Bigger shoulders. Older shoulders.

Drove the big two-ton grain truck in the field – huge, endless fields of grain; thousands of acres out and out so they seemed to reach into the sky – and watched the farmer on the combine, and when the hopper on the combine was full, he drove the truck under the hopper's auger spout and they augered the grain out the spout into the back of the truck. A stream of grain six inches thick and flowing like it was alive. Gold, rich living gold filling the truck. Chaff and dust off the combine blowing in his eyes and nose so thick it made him sneeze and spit and itch like the dust was made of tiny needles. But still a wonder to see, to put your hand in and feel the grain pouring. Still a wonder.

When the grain truck was full, it had to be driven into a little town four miles down a dusty road and emptied into a grain elevator to be shipped out by railroad on the tracks that went by the elevator. First time the farmer drove, but after that he let the kid go alone while he stayed and kept combining because the weather was good and you never knew. Never knew when it might go bad. Rain to ruin the wheat. Or bad wind to knock the grain off the plants so the combine couldn't pick it up. You never knew. Had to keep going. And the kid drove the truck out to the dirt road and into the town and onto the grate next to the elevator and dumped the grain out the back and into the grate. Raising the dump bed as it ran out to make it flow. And then lower the bed and back, empty, to the field just in time to catch up with the farmer on the combine, which had another full hopper to dump.

So tired by the end of the day that he was dizzy. Had trouble walking. Or chewing food. Or even remembering how bad it was back home. Back Home. Blind tired so that he crawled across the truck seat and slept there, on the rough seat, rather than the sack bunk in the equipment shed. Tired. So tired.

But he got her done.

By God.

The tractor was easier, but in some ways more difficult. When the grain harvest was done, the field had to be ploughed by a two-bladed plough that cut and curve-flopped the black soil over on itself like folded cake. Long field – two to three hundred acres, half mile long. The farmer did the first round to make the furrow straight, up and back down with two furrows, one in the middle and one to the side, then the boy took it. Just follow the furrow to the end – took a half hour sitting on the big M Farmall pulling out in front of the plough, waving the seagulls away when hundreds came to eat the earthworms the plough turned up. Seagull poop everywhere, on the tractor, all over him, the plough and – worse –

219

on the hot muffler out in front of him so thick blue-green smoke came back to him in a hot fog, bringing the smell of burned poop, almost sticky, around and into his mouth and nose and eyes and ears. Burned bird crap, that he knew – *knew* – he would smell and taste to the end of his life.

A small break from the gulls at the end of the field while he pulled the trip rope and trip-raised the plough, turned the tractor out in a wide circle, moved the tractor over and started back in the second furrow, dropped the plough blades down and settled in the seat to once more get covered by the gulls.

But not for long. Not for long. Because one day he turned and looked back down at the end of the field and saw the farmer standing next to a county sheriff's car and knew he couldn't avoid them. He thought of running, but knew that wouldn't work. And so the same thing again.

Detained. The farmer paid him with a twenty-dollar bonus, and the deputy took him to a town fifty miles away. Bought him a hamburger and a chocolate malt and then turned him over to another church volunteer. The boy wondered how there could be volunteers wherever you seemed to be – thought they must be getting paid for taking him back – but this one was a little different. Thin, tall, chain-smoked while he drove, lighting one cigarette with another, ashes down his front, didn't talk about Jesus. Didn't talk at all. Just by God drove. Steady fifty miles an hour in a '49 Ford until he got to the boy's home, dropped him off, turned, and drove away in a cloud of blue-grey cigarette smoke. Not a word.

Back.

But it was late in the day and the two of them were well drunk, fighting drunk, sloppy drunk, and didn't even know he'd come back. So he turned, moving away from them and the grim aspect of the apartment building. Like a prison. Like the death-house walls left by the Japanese soldiers where they'd slaughtered civilians, which he'd seen in 1946 when he lived on the streets of Manila as a seven-year-old boy. Stains on the rock walls there where the women and children were lined up and killed with flamethrowers. Light from the apartment building – like it made its own off-yellow puke-coloured light that seemed to smell. Bad stains. Bad light. Bad smell.

Away from that.

He still had food in his belly – a leftover taste and feeling from the hamburger and chocolate malt – and it was dusk, not dark yet, but soft grey moving close to hard dark. All right if he kept out of sight along the sides of buildings in shadows, so he moved down the alleys and slid, shadow to shadow, to the library to think on what to do next.

Safe.

THE PLAN

So he was thirteen.

And he fully intended to run.

To Run. In his heart and mind, he could feel it. Run so far and long and deep they would never find him. Run and get a job somewhere, anywhere. Get food. Sleep where he could. He remembered crawling into the centre of tyres on a rack by a closed garage to sleep one night when he was hitchhiking. Rough edges cutting him, but off the ground and he slept hard enough to dream. He could always find a place to sleep. Some food and a place to sleep.

He planned it. To Run and never be brought back

again now that he was thirteen. Clean away – forever away. It was coming on summer now and there would be work at farms or – and he dreamt at times of this – at a ranch even further west. West. Be a cowboy and work cattle on a horse. He could see that, see himself as a cowboy. Get the hat, and boots with a design stitched on them, an eagle stitched in red thread on a black boot. He'd herd cattle on a horse named – he couldn't think of a name. In all the movies, Roy Rogers had a horse named Trigger. Gene Autry rode Champion. Something like that. Get a horse and name him . . . something. He'd get a good name for a horse and be a cowboy and herd cattle and save – he didn't know what, but in the grainy black-and-white movies they usually saved ranches or pretty girls or small towns. So he'd do that. Run far west – West – be a cowboy and ride wherever he wanted, when he wanted.

But first he would Run. Absolutely first. Get away again.

Except.

Except he didn't.

Couldn't.

Couldn't run.

And at first he could not tell why. Everything was perfect for running. School was out, summer was coming – not, he thought, that school mattered for him. It worked for others. Didn't work for him. Teachers said things he was supposed to hear and handed him work to study, but he didn't hear or couldn't study, because he had to think about other things. How he was a stranger in the class. With the wrong clothes, the wrong hair, pimples on his forehead. Wrong family. No family. Family that hooked him off and down so hard it made him a freak to other kids in school. Should have been in a circus where people paid a quarter to come in a sideshow tent and see the kid who never fit in. He came from a bad family and that was what was wrong. When he thought of it at all, he would think how everybody in the school either didn't notice him or, if they did, they laughed at him. Grey-green thoughts like the seagull poop off the hot muffler. He never thought about school except to know it was a nightmare walking.

Still, summer was coming, and there would be work out in the North Dakota farms or further west – West – where he could try to get work as a cowboy on a ranch.

They wouldn't even know he was gone, really. They'd sit in their whiskey-wine-beer fog and not have a thought of him. Think he was fishing in the river or gone to the woods. Why think about a worthless kid at all? They didn't know him, really. He was as much a stranger there as he was at school. Easy to leave and not look back.

A week passed, and then another week, and he did his normal life, normal days. No, not normal. Routine. That's it. Settled into the routine of his regular life.

Once they passed out, he slept in the back seat of the '51 Chevy coupe they had but never drove since they could walk to the liquor store. Stretch out across the seat like a fabric bed and doze. Risky if they came outside. Which they almost never did, but you never knew. Never knew.

Or, if they were still awake and conscious, he would head down to the dark basement of the old apartment building. Back behind the coal-fired furnace, he had dragged an old easy chair he found in a corner of the basement. Tattered. Stuffing coming out. Wire springs poking up. But comfortable for all that, soft and comfortable, and he could settle back in and down and fall asleep. Warm in the winter with the furnace going, and cool in the summer with the furnace shut down next to the dark and cool-damp basement walls.

He had a hot plate down there, in a corner on an old woodbox, with a wire up to the outlet on the side of the bare bulb that lit up with red-hot wire filaments. And a pot and an ancient toaster that would do one slice of bread at a time. The door on the side of the toaster flopped down to let the slice of bread slide down so it could be turned over and the little door closed to toast the other side against the glowing hot-red wires.

Some evenings he would get a whole loaf of white bread and a jar of peanut butter, and eat toast and peanut butter sitting in the chair. Crunchy with bits of nuts if he could get it, but creamy if that's all he could find upstairs when they passed out. He liked that he could get more to chew with crunchy peanut butter. Now and then he would get some salty butter, and mix it with the peanut butter, spread thick on the bread, and now and then a jar of grape jam – he had to buy or swipe it himself and he didn't like buying because it was expensive and stealing was risky because he might get caught and because it put him out in stores in the daylight when

227

and where he wasn't safe. He'd eat peanut-butter-and-grape-jam slices until he was so full he felt like a wood tick. It would be perfect if he could get a small carton of milk to wash it down. Perfect.

When he was really hungry, which seemed almost all the time, he could eat a whole loaf except for slices of bread he had to throw to the rats so they would leave him alone.

He didn't mind the rats here. They were small. The rats he had seen on the outskirts of bombed and gutted Manila when he was just a kid had been huge. Those rats looked like small dogs. They said the rats fed on the bodies of dead Japanese soldiers that had been buried in caves with bulldozers and that was why they were so big. And fat. He didn't know that for certain, although he'd crawled into a small cave once and seen the bodies and their rusted rifles and rotten clothing and grinning skulls, and he wished to God he'd never gone into the cave. He'd crawled to get in there, and then he crawled out so fast he must have been a blur, and he didn't sleep right for a month and longer. Still bothered him when he thought of the skulls. He'd seen big rats, but hadn't seen them eating the bodies. Might have happened, though.

You never knew. They were huge, and if they piled on, it might not take them long to finish off a whole body. They were big enough.

These rats were small, and when they figured out that he wasn't dangerous, they accepted him and, in the end, would sit up on their back legs and beg when he was eating toast and peanut butter. My family, he thought once, sitting there watching them beg for food. My family of begging rats. Well hell, he thought, why not? Better than what he had.

Along with the hot plate and pot, he had picked up an old sheet-metal frying pan with a diamond shape stamped into the handle and words stamp-printed that read MADE IN CLEVELAND. A little rusty, but he worked off the rust and stain with steel wool, and it was all right. Sometimes he would cook a small piece of meat in the pan, frying it with sliced raw potatoes cooked in the meat's own fat, and sprinkled with grains of coarse salt. Sop the juice up with a piece of white bread folded over and chew slowly, slow and easy. Made his mouth water just thinking about it.

Up in the morning. Either in the car or basement if he was in town and not out in the woods or upstream along the river. Eat a cold piece of bread with peanut butter wiped on it. Once, during the winter, he'd been upstairs when they were both passed out and he'd found a can of corned beef, which he could never afford to buy on his own. Square can with a key winder on the side to roll a strip of metal to open it and he ate the whole can for breakfast. Wiped the greasy inside of the can with his finger and sucked the taste off, mostly fat and strip meat, the fat melting in his mouth and meat sliding down into his stomach. Memory food. Like the steak the farmer had bought him at a cafe in North Dakota when they took in the last load of grain before the sheriff came when he was ploughing and he was not arrested, but detained. Steak so good he ate the fat rimming the sides and wiped the plate with a piece of bread and sucked the burn-taste off the bone. Wished he had it again. Every day. Memory food. Like handfuls of sticky white rice with a dime can of oily sardines dumped on it in Manila on the streets. To be hungry, a young kid really tight hungry, alongside the blown-apart buildings, and have somebody give him the rice on a piece of cardboard and an opened can of sardines. Drink off the juice and put the sardines on the rice and stir it with his fingers and swallow without chewing. Lick the cardboard free of salty fish oil. Longtime memory food. Carry the memory forever.

So up from sleep, and eat what he could for a breakfast, and then out into the town. Daylight so he had to be careful. Moving down side streets and through alleys. He had a rusty old Hiawatha bike, no fenders, a slightly bent carrying rack on back, rattles from a loose chain, and wobbly wheels with loose spokes. But when he was in town, the bike helped him get around a little faster. In Manila, he'd had an old Japanese military bike like Rom's. Painted black with symbols he couldn't read on a piece of tin riveted to the front tube that led down to the fork. Rear rack made of rusty welded pipe and fat tyres that were always leaking air. But he awkwardly learned to ride a two-wheeler even though it was too big for him because he was a small kid. The bike helped him get around the city for a little while before somebody stole it. He didn't feel that bad because the tyres were always getting flat and he'd have to find somebody with a tyre pump. Besides, he had learned to catch rides with soldiers in jeeps and trucks when he had to move any distance.

If it was late spring or early summer, which it was now – his birthday taking him into thirteen was in the middle of May – the fish would be running up the river to spawn. They'd get caught below the small power dam by steel grates where they couldn't get around or over. He'd watch as they circled in large surging pools of turbulent muddy water until they were so tired the rushing current would take them back downstream where the water was still and they could rest and clear the mud from their gills before they tried again.

The fish didn't eat when they were spawning, so fishing for them with bait didn't work. But he'd found they could be snagged with the right kind of hook.

He had a corner in the back of the basement where he hid things he didn't want his parents or anybody else to take. Private things. His old lemonwood bow with a leather-wrapped handgrip and rawhide backing and arrows he made from second-grade cedar shafts he got for a quarter each from a catalogue – along with a cheap fletcher to glue feathers on with model aeroplane glue and plastic nocks for a nickel each to take the corded string on the bow. A cutoff sleeve from an old leather jacket he saw in the alley rubbish that he sewed into a shoulder quiver with nylon fishline – sixty-pound test – and a finger tab made from old boot leather cut to the shape of his fingers. Points for the arrows were expensive, but he found that empty .38 cartridge cases would glue on just right and made good blunts to take small animals. He knew the cops carried .38 revolvers and they were familiar with him from the times he ran off, so they gave him a box of fired brass collected from the shooting range. Fifty in a box. Enough to last him his whole life. They'd take down grouse, rabbits, big grey squirrels if he caught one low on a tree. If they were too high up, he didn't shoot because if he missed – and he did, often, shooting up – the arrow would go past the squirrel and out of sight, lost in the woods.

In the corner with the bow, he kept his fishing gear, too. An old spring-steel rod with a still older Shakespeare sturdy baitcasting reel filled with the heavy fishline. No sport there. Heavy cord and steel leaders. Not fly fishing for ten-inch fish. Fishing gear was for taking meat, catching food, and you never knew what size fish you might get in the muddy river. An ugly rig, strong, but not good for snagging.

Had to touch, feel the line, when snagging. The

snagging setup was a short, thick line wrapped around a stick of wood – not over thirty feet – and a heavy steel leader clipped hard to a large, specially sharpened treble hook. The hook had to sink in the roiling water below the dam, but this was still too light, even as heavy as it was, so he hardwired a large sinker or a steel railroad bolt-nut beneath the hook and out of the way.

He took the snagging gear from the hiding place and made his way on the old Hiawatha bicycle to the power dam through alleys and back streets, clunking and rattling. Above the spillway at the bottom of the dam was a stand of brush. Thick willows with early leaves. He hid the bike in the willows. Ugly as it was, he didn't think anybody would steal it, but . . . just that. But. Hide it anyway. He'd hang back in the willows himself to watch the dam and spillway until he was sure. Nobody else was there – the boys who had big shoulders and tried to hurt him never came down to the dam. They didn't fish, but . . . But. Had to think on it all the time to stay safe. The workers inside the dam mostly either went into town for beer or stayed inside the brick building drinking coffee, playing draughts or five-card gin rummy. They never looked down at the spillway. The water was gone by then, had worked through the dam. Why look at it?

When it was clear, he went down to the concrete ledge over the spillway and unwound the snagging line, lowering it over the water. He scraped his fingers on the concrete to make them more sensitive, and swung the snag hook forward up the current to drop into the water and drift back in the flowing depths next to the wall.

Snagging was an art.

The fish, trying to swim upstream against the rushing water coming from the spillway, worked tight along the wall where it was easier to swim. You swung the hook forward, set it down in the water, let it slide back against the concrete wall until you felt it bump something.

Nose of a fish.

Pull up sharply, quickly, set the hook in the lower jaw, and pull the fish hand over hand. Not a sport, this was not a hobby. You needed strength to take fish for food.

No art there. Slide and jerk and you caught a fish. Big whoop.

The art came in knowing what kind of fish you were snagging. Carp swam at the same time as other fish, mixed in. But nobody wanted carp, they were too bony and lived on the bottom in the mud. The meat was soft and tasted muddy, people said, so he never ate one. Somebody told him they ate carp in China. Fried them whole in a sheet-metal bowl over an open fire. Left the scales on and the guts inside. Picked the meat out of the bones by hand. But he didn't know whether it was true or not; for sure, nobody here wanted them or ate them. People here wanted walleyes and northern pike. Mostly large walleyes so they could cut fillets off the side. Eat the cheeks and eyes. Good meat.

Walleyes and northern pike had hard noses, tough bone jaws out in front. Carp had soft noses, spongy mouths and lips, sucker mouths for feeding on the bottom.

Swing the hook forward and let it slide back. Fishline across the finger rough-sanded on the concrete to make it more sensitive. Feel it. Feel it slide along the concrete. When it hit a fish front, the line would hesitate, the hook would bounce a little. Just a touch on the line and, if it was a soft bounce, let it roll off to the side. Felt it through the touchy finger – soft bounce meant a bottom-feeder mudfish.

Harder hit, really hard hit – a kind of click-hit and a jerk-up – and you knew you had a northern or walleye under the jaw. Pull him up, swing hard and up on the bank behind you, and you had food. Fillets with tiny Y-bones to pick out and spit away if it was a northern. Clean white-meat fillets if it was a walleye.

This time, this early summer when he was just thirteen, in the middle of the morning, it was a walleye. Five, maybe six pounds. Good-size male, a golden brown on his sides. But this morning it was not for food, not food for him at any rate.

He had a deal with the Northern Lights saloon, which he first approached mainly because his parents never drank there so no one knew who they, or he, were. Elmer Peterson was an old Swede who had owned the bar as long as the boy was alive and more, more years than the boy knew. They had what the boy called a deal and Elmer called an arrangement. Elmer had such a thick Swedish accent the word seemed to trip coming out of his mouth. But the old man liked to use the word, like it made him something more than he thought he was, and it made the boy smile every time he heard it. Made him smile every time Elmer tried to use big English words.

The Northern Lights had empty three-pound coffee cans along the bar floor for spittoons, and sawdust on the floor in case men missed the coffee cans with tobacco juice. No stools. Men, rough men, men who worked the river for logging below the dam or drove yellow bulldozers and graders on the road crews, drank standing at the bar. Just beer. But a lot of it. Drank until they were ready to fall down. The bar had a raised wooden handrail along the front edge, and men would hold that rail with one hand and drink with the other, spitting on the floor or into the coffee cans. Hold the rail until it didn't keep them up any longer and then stagger over to some plank benches in the rear to sleep – pass out, really – until they had slept it off and could walk to leave.

It was here he took the walleye. Anytime he caught a fish too big to cook in the basement on the hot plate, he took it to the Northern Lights bar, where he had the arrangement with Elmer. The bar had an ancient cooler in the back and Elmer would pay the boy for the fish and put them on ice in the cooler to sell to his patrons. Elmer left the guts in the fish to keep the weight up and the meat good. Gut them, and it made them lighter and the meat dried from the inside, and the patrons wanted bigger fish with soft, moist fresh meat. Heavier fish. That's what he called them. His patrons. Except it came out 'patroons'.

Not the men drinking standing at the bar. They weren't his patrons. They didn't pay for fish. If they wanted fish, they would get their own. And if they wanted to cut their drunk down early by eating, Elmer had a grill in the back of the bar he kept hot and greased from a five-gallon metal bucket of lard on the floor. Kept a lid on that bucket so nobody could spit in it.

On the grill, Elmer cooked thin, stamped-out meat patties in thick hot lard. Swore they were beef, but the boy had eaten them once and didn't believe they were beef. Could have been anything. Like in Manila when he ate meat on rice off pieces of cardboard. Could be dog, maybe. Or sheep. Surely wasn't beef. Elmer wiped small, thin buns in the grease next to the meat until the buns were burned black-brown and dripping grease. He slapped the meat between the two buns, dropped it hot and smoking on a piece of ripped-square day-old news-paper on the bar, and held out his hand.

Quarter and a dime. Thirty-five cents. Hamburger for a quarter and a dime. Most of the men didn't eat them, didn't want to slow their drunk, but Elmer kept the grease bucket and off-meat burgers for the same reason he kept the fish in the cooler – the patrons.

Tourists.

Word of the saloon spread. Men, and sometimes men with women, came to fish the river above the dam for the legendary muskies. Said they went up to fifty pounds, though the boy had never heard of one that big being caught. Still, they came from cities and sometimes even other states, towing their boats on trailers, and almost all of them wanted to see the Northern Lights saloon.

Place drew them like flies. They thought the saloon was what they called local colour. Something to see and take home. The bar was too dark to take pictures and Elmer wouldn't have let them anyway, so it had to be enough to just sit and see, get a beer and eat an off-meat burger on a smoke-fired, greasy bun, and see the men standing at the bar drinking.

There were two seedy booths against the wall opposite the bar. Phony leather seats covered in puke stains and worse. Chipped and stained and whittle-carved wooden tables coming out from the wall where the tourists could sit and drink a pony-piss beer and eat a grease-bomb burger off a piece of dirty newspaper. Then go home and brag about how tough they were to have been there. How grimy it had been, greasy. Local colour.

Most of the patrons knew about boats on trailers and beer and expensive fishing gear, but they didn't know how to fish. They wanted something for pictures, something to take home and brag about at the office, maybe cook on their backyard barbecues.

And Elmer would wait until they had eaten a grease-bomb burger and drunk a pony-piss beer or two and then mention he had a fish caught that morning back in the cooler.

Didn't matter when it was actually caught, Elmer always told them it was caught just that morning. Big northern, walleye, musky. Whatever he had – caught that morning if somebody-anybody wanted to take it home. Elmer could get five, six, seven dollars, maybe ten dollars, per fish from the patrons. If it was a big walleye with gold-brown sides and fat cheeks, ten dollars easy. A man makes forty dollars a week working at a factory, ten dollars was a lot of money. But it was a lot of fish. A lot of bragging rights. Show a picture of the fish back home, and the brag would last a long time. Good investment for a ten spot.

Sometimes, with a good-size fish, Elmer would give the boy two dollars. Gave him that now – two dollars for a five-pound walleye with golden sides.

Two dollars in his pocket. Along with the money he had saved and scrounged, this brought him to over five dollars. Five dollars and sixty cents. Big money. Kept money if he didn't get caught by the big kids and they took it.

Travelling money.

But still he didn't run. He wanted to run, but didn't. Somehow couldn't run. He dreamt of it sleeping in the chair near the furnace, of leaving, finding work, being a cowboy.

But he only left in his dreams.

Which wasn't like him. He didn't sit and dream when he could be going, like he had some big plan to think on.

He went, instead, to the woods, along the river,

where he'd build a fire and catch some bullheads on worms and fry them in the frying pan and eat them crispy and good. Get a loaf of bread for twenty cents and sop up the hot juice with soft bread.

And think. He always thought better in the woods along the river. Where it was safe. Once he was in the woods, folded into the forest, nobody could catch him. No one bothered him.

The woods was a good place to think.

On why he wasn't running.

THINKING ON THINGS

It was still daylight, so moving was risky.

He kept to the alleys until he came near the railroad yards where there were bad dwellings, where the hard kids lived near the north end of the railroad yards, past the roundhouse, in ugly grey houses. Almost black from all the years when the rail lines used coal-fired locomotives pushing out smoky soot. Looked like a picture of hell, like Manila and the stains on the wall. All the houses by the railroad yards needed a coat of paint. And more. Scrubbing first, then paint, and then move. No place to live, these Hell houses. Rough houses, rough people down by the yards. That's how people spoke when they talked of that area, those people, at all. Said they were coarse people who lived down by the yards. Like it explained everything about them.

He didn't live down by the yards, but anybody who saw how he lived would call him the same. Coarse. Parents were drunks and their kid was always in the streets and alleys. 'Coarse'; it was a good word. No matter how he felt, thought, he was cut from some of the same rough cloth.

Thing was, he had to cross the railroad yards to get down to the Sixth Street bridge, which led out of town going north to where the woods started. Woods that didn't end ever, but kept going north. He looked on a large map once at the library and there was nothing but woods all the way up into Canada, like the forest went all the way north to Hudson Bay.

The woods led north, pulled him north to where it was safe.

But to get there, he had to cross the yards, jump over three sets of rails and a low fence, and then make it another two blocks to the Sixth Street bridge. Another quarter mile after that, he moved off the road and then into the trees. Moved through the low brush like a knife through water. Opened in front of him, closed behind him, nobody could see him. He was there, and then he was not there. Like he'd never been there. Clean gone. Disappeared.

But first he had to cross the tracks.

And it was still daylight. He'd have to be careful, be still and watch before he made his move. He sat by the back of an old equipment shed along the tracks and studied everything ahead of him. Forty yards across the tracks would put him by the old coal tower where they used to load coal into the coal tenders behind the loco-motives. Now it was a roost for a hundred or so pigeons. He used to climb inside at night with a small torch and take a couple of pigeons now and then when he couldn't get anything hunting in the woods. He'd grab them off the cross members in the tower and break their necks. *Click*. Then he'd clean them and cook them, boiled in a battered aluminium saucepan he'd found in the rubbish over the hot plate in the basement. Not a lot of meat, but good. Like dark meat on a chicken or a smaller grouse breast. Good taste. Somebody said once they served them in fancy restaurants in the cities. Didn't call them pigeons because nobody would eat them. Called them squabs. Call them that – squabs – and people paid top dollar for them. Didn't know any better, didn't know they were eating pigeon. He stripped the meat off the bones when they were boiled, and ate the meat with a little salt rolled in a tube of white bread. Made his mouth water now, thinking about it, watching the pigeons flying around the tower before they went in to roost. But he'd already decided to go to the woods, build a fire, and catch a bullhead or two or three to cook on a stick over the fire. Keep thinking on why he hadn't run yet, sitting in smoke to keep the mosquitoes down, eating the red fish meat off the bullheads. If he didn't make meat that way, he'd come back after dark and take a couple of pigeons back to his basement hidey-hole. Boil them and have a late snack. Bread and pigeon. Call it squab and he'd be a high-tone man. Nothing coarse about a man who eats squab.

Forty yards to the coal tower. If he made it that far, he could hide in the shadows until he made sure it was clear to move again. He stayed low and moved behind a row of more equipment sheds until he was at the bridge. Then thirty or so yards to the bridge. Across the bridge and off the road into the forest and done and gone.

He was ready to move. All clear and he jumped out over the tracks and was almost at the coal tower when he heard a yell behind him to the right. He took a quick look while picking up speed. He ran with his arms reaching ahead for more land with each stride.

A kid named Mikey thundered behind him. Fifteen or sixteen years old and built like a freakish gorilla with long arms and sloping forehead covered with little red freckles and short reddish hair. He was a tough nut who wore heavy high-top work shoes with thick soles. He liked to kick a kid when he was down – had, in fact, caught the boy two, three months ago behind the bakery, leaving bruises and sore ribs that still hadn't entirely healed. The woman at the bakery, nice woman, left two or three hot fresh rolls out for him on some mornings. He ate them still warm from the big oven.

Mikey had two of his brothers with him. Both a little younger, but still big. Kyle and Pudge. Funny names, but mean kids, looking like slightly smaller Mikeys. He took a bad beating that time. Went down and rolled in a ball, but they kicked at him while he was down. Kicked his ribs and his stomach so hard he puked up the rolls.

Mikey was alone this time, wearing big clodhopper

boots at the end of those heavy legs, and there was no way Mikey could catch him.

He found a little more speed as he cut between the equipment sheds in his cheap high-top tennis shoes – PF Flyers – advertised in *Boys' Life* magazine. They weren't cool, but they were light on his feet and he made two steps for every one of Mikey's, and it wasn't long before the big clunker realized he was wasting time and slowed and then stopped. Gave up.

He dropped back to a fast trot as he cleared the equipment sheds and approached the bridge. Not even breathing hard. Crossed the bridge, worked his way along the road, and then slid off the side into the woods like he was going home. Which he was, he thought, smiling. Going home.

One time the three brothers, with another bogey-eating jackass named Harvey, had hidden waiting for him and almost caught him at the bridge. They'd jumped out of an old rusty car body in the ditch where they were hiding and followed him into the trees, into his home. He smiled now, thinking about it. He disappeared on them. Just folded into the trees and willows and disappeared clean. They spread out to search for him, but he lay down and slithered into and under tall swamp grass the way deer sometimes hid from hunters, and they passed not fifteen yards from him and didn't even know he was there. He thought of standing up and yelling at them and getting them to follow him deeper into the woods. Still deeper until . . . He wasn't sure. Until they were lost, maybe. Lost and not knowing what to do and he could get one of them alone and . . .

And nothing.

Just stay away from them. Let them be. That was the best. He cut into the thickest part of the trees and worked back out to the edge of the river where it curved around a big, lazy bend, an eddy, a place where the water swirled into a constant dead hole. He called it his magic spot because he knew the bullheads stayed there feeding on the bottom, which they felt with their whiskers.

Further south, way south, they were called catfish and they were huge, fifty, sixty pounds. But up here they were called bullheads and they stayed small. Even big ones rarely made two pounds, and smaller bullheads at half a pound, or just over one pound, were the most common. Still tasted good. He had to be careful holding

251

them, getting them off the hook. They had sharp spines on their front fins and back that went into your hand like needles. They left a poison slime in the hole that hurt like blazes and got swollen and could make your hand and sometimes your whole arm stiff and hard to use.

But good meat. Reddish-dark meat that was rich, good food. No trout in his river – too muddy – but people said the bullhead meat was as good as brook trout caught fresh in the mountains. Some day he'd fish those mountains. Catch a trout and see for himself if it was as good as bullheads. Maybe sooner than later if he ever decided to run.

His brain started on its own, thinking on running away, on why he didn't seem to be running. He shook his head. That was for later. Now he had to get a line in the water, gather dry wood, make a fire. He jerked his mind back to catching something to eat, maybe a bull-head or two. They were easy to catch. He'd think more after he ate.

He kept a strand of fishline with a leader and hook and lead sinker attached to a willow pole hidden by the eddy back in the brush. Looked just like another willow if somebody saw it, but nobody came there anyway. Not to his woods. Sometimes he actually felt like he owned them, like it was his house, his room. He found the pole now. He flipped over a rotten log and pulled out a couple of earthworms before they could slick-slither fast back into the moist dirt. He gang-slopped both of them in a gob of loops on the hook and then swung the line out over the water so the hook dropped on the bottom where the bullheads fed. They worked their head feelers around in the mud for food, and if they felt the worms, they tried to take them and they were his. Easy to catch.

It was coming on dusk now. He made a small smoke fire – which called to mind images of Sig on the riverbank – to discourage the mosquitoes, then gathered wood for a proper fire before it got dark night.

Night.

He liked the night in the woods, but he knew some people who didn't.

Thought there were monsters. Hear a mouse rustling in the grass and think of something big. Mean. Bears or panthers. He'd seen bears, lots of them, but never a panther. One of the uncles he'd stayed with once told him they were there, could walk without sound the way an owl could fly in silence. He asked the uncle why people were afraid of sounds if the panther walked without it, and the uncle told him to quit being a smart-aleck kid or he'd probably be eaten by a panther some dark night.

But he liked the night. Because he was part of it. Or night was part of him. The darkness folded around him like the woods and it was like being a bigger safety. Double safe. Maybe even more than that. He'd learned to like the dark in Manila, where the enemy had destroyed all the power-generating machines when they killed everybody and gutted the city. Even after the American army dragged the abandoned enemy sub to the city docks, ran wires from it, and used it as a temporary generator for some emergency lights, the city was mostly dark, and it was a different city in the dark. Not quite so safe, things happened outside the limits of being safe, dark things that no man should see or even know about and he was only a little kid but he saw and knew and he would never forget. Never get it out of his brain-pictures. But all that had taught him how to move in the dark, in the ruins and alleys, and the dark became a tool he could use to not be there. Had white-blond hair, but he covered it with a dark green army field cap a soldier gave him, a cap so big it came down and rested on his ears, bent them down a little. Soldier said he looked like Dumbo, who was an elephant with big ears. A mean soldier joke. But his cap hid the hair.

And then he could vanish in the dark. Clean and gone. Like now.

He brought in more wood and built the fire up. Felt the fishline going into the water, pulled it a bit, and knew he had a fish on. Easy to catch. He pulled the line in and he'd caught nearly a two-pounder. Bullheads had no scales. Just skin. One of the larger ones like this had golden skin on its belly. He took the fish off the hook slowly, avoiding the sharp spines by the front fins. Using dry grass he wiped off the slime, then gutted the fish with the small pocketknife he always carried. Because you never knew. Never knew. He threw the guts back in the river for other fish and crayfish to eat, and cut a small forked willow that he whittled and sharpened to make a meat spit. He slid the bullhead on the two sharpened prongs and held it over the fire, but not too close. Didn't want to completely torch the meat. But not too far either. Close enough to cook it and crackle the skin, which was as good as the meat, even better if it was rolled in cracker crumbs and fried in grease. But still good this way. Hunger made food better.

The fish cooked fast. Ten minutes, five on each side, and it was done. He sat back by the fire and ate the skin first, peeled it with his fingers, before picking the meat off. It was hot, but it cooled fast and didn't take him long to eat it all. Put the bony carcass and head back in the water at the side of the river. Slow current here and an easy spot for the crayfish to get at and eat the remains.

He added more wood on the fire to get a good-size blaze. He needed good smoke to keep the bugs down.

He lay back on the grass. Good food, but still not full; there should have been more grease and some white bread. Still, the meal was good and it cut the edge of his hunger. He wasn't packed full, but he'd caught and cooked and eaten good food.

He looked at the stars, spread across the sky like they'd been painted there, and he thought about how each of them was supposed to be a sun and maybe even had planets around it. He'd read that the number of stars was so big they couldn't be counted, more stars than all the grains of sand on all the beaches in the world. He'd also read that if you weighed all the ants on earth in one place, they would weigh more than all the people in one place.

Crazy.

But there was a farmer's pile of stars. And ants wherever you looked. So you never knew. You just never knew.

And then it came to him. Out of nowhere, while his brain was full of thoughts flopping around like fish. Stars, ants, bullheads, grease, bread. Outrunning Mikey, big, slow-footed Mikey. How nice it would have been to have not just white bread, but two or three of those hot fresh rolls from the bakery to eat with the bullhead meat while he counted stars and thought of ants and wondered how many ants it would take to weigh the same as him. How many ants would it take to weigh the same as a big, slow-footed monster like Mikey.

And it was right there.

Right in the middle of his swirling thoughts.

It was the library.

The reason he didn't run away now when he came on thirteen and it was a perfect time for running was the library.

No. Not exactly. Not only the library.

It was the library and the librarian.

But still more than that. It wasn't the library, as much as the librarian.

THE LIBRARY

Big old bugger of a building. Solid brick with carved stone over the entry doors that read: CARNEGIE. Old, with high windows that let in shafted sunlight so everything looked like it was made of gold. Square windowpanes that seemed to channel the shafts of gold light filled with dust motes. And all around were stacks and stacks of books against the walls, with freestanding shelves in the middle of the rooms filled with more books. On the left as he came in was a high flat rack with magazines and newspapers against the wall and, in front of that, large oak tables with straight-back oak chairs. Light shone down on the dark oak of the tables so they seemed alive.

Deep oak colour in the light-like-living wood.

And quiet. No hard sounds. Just smooth quiet.

Place smelt like wood and what? Smelt like . . . books. Official-looking wood-book-smelling quiet place that made you relax the minute you came in the door.

That's what made it feel safe. An official government place where nobody would mess with you. A safe place where none of the loud-hard kids would come.

A kind place.

That was it. An official kind place. Big building with gold light on oak tables where you could be safe.

But North Dakota was safe as well. As safe as the library. Even more because, once he ran west, he was far from all the bad things that tracked him now. Away from the hard ones, away from his parent-vipers, where he could move in daylight and not have to run in alleys.

Still he stayed.

Even though he knew it was safer working farms in North Dakota – especially now that he could drive the big grain dump trucks and the big diesel tractor for ploughing that made his shoulders bigger.

And yet he stayed.

And he knew, even as he worked his brain around it, that the real reason he had not run away this time wasn't just the library.

It was the library *and* the librarian.

She was a grown-up. And he had no luck with grown-ups. Couldn't really count on what they said, what they did. They always seemed to say one thing, promise one thing, and wham, go ahead and do something else. You could never make a plan on what they said or did, couldn't even make sense of it.

He thought of Manila and the war. No sense at all to ruin a city that had been as pretty as Manila. No sense to kill all those people and gut the city and leave ugly stains on the wall where they had made people stand before they turned the flames on them. He couldn't see kids doing any of that, just enemy soldier grown-ups. For nothing. Not a single good reason in the world.

And the librarian was a grown-up.

Why would he stay for a grown-up? She was nice to him. But other grown-ups had been nice to him, and then, when he relaxed his guard, they turned not so nice.

So it didn't make sense that he would stay for the librarian.

Even though she . . . she was different.

He'd been cutting through an alley on a cold day the previous winter – minus twenty – when it was just dark. Late afternoon, early evening, really, far too soon for the drunks to be loose in the bars where he would pretend to sell newspapers for fifteen cents each, and when they weren't looking close, he'd sweep some of their change off the bar by accident. Change fell on the floor and he'd pick it up for them and keep some of it. Maybe a quarter. Couple of dimes. On a good night he might make one, maybe two bucks.

It was too early to run the bars for change.

And it was cold.

Blue cold. That's how he thought of it. Walk with one ear pressed down in the collar of your jacket until the other ear got numb. Then switch ears. Left, right. Numb, flip ears, numb.

Blue cold.

He'd come to the end of the alley, and between two buildings, he'd seen the front of the library. Probably looked at it a hundred times without actually seeing it at all. This time it looked different with the steam-fog hanging in front of it so the light looked blurry. Special, like movie light.

The library looked warm.

And it was blue cold outside.

And he had some time before he could work the bars so why not the library?

It surprised him that he'd never been inside before. Maybe it had always seemed too much like school. Or a grown-up trap, where he'd get cornered and they had him because there was only one door.

But it was cold.

And the light from the front of the library cut through the ice fog and looked warm.

So warm.

He moved to the door, opened it, and went inside.

Not what he expected at all. Bright and quiet and smelt of wood and books and a gentle flower smell – perfume or lotion.

Smelt of being kind.

And it was warm.

God, it was warm. He could feel the warmth driving the cold in his jacket into his body. He unzipped the jacket and let the warm in, which pushed the cold out.

He looked around and he realized with a small jolt that the tables nearby were filled with old ladies. Eight or ten of them. Really old. Some of them had to be eighty. That's where the smell was coming from – the ladies. They sat around the tables with blue hair and glasses and old dresses, knitting balls of yarn into sweaters or scarves and mittens, and the lotion smell came from them. Gentle and kind, grandmother smells. He loved his grandmother, who was the best grown-up of all. She smelt of lotion. When he was very small, he had lived with her for a time, one summer during the war. She made him apple pies and rubbed his knees when they hurt at night and held him when he cried because he was missing his mother, who was working at a war plant in Chicago. Then he was sent to join his mother, and his grandmother went north to work on the cook camp for the road-building crew.

He didn't cry any more; he'd quit crying in Manila because nothing that happened in his life was as bad as what happened to the women and kids in Manila when they stood next to that wall. Not even when his mother was crazy-out-of-her-brain drunk and tried to stab him with a butcher knife under the kitchen table. She didn't know what she was doing and he never even got clipped. He moved too fast and kept the chair and table legs in front of him. Her knife clinked on the shiny chair legs when it hit the metal. He didn't like it at all, but it still wasn't nearly as bad as Manila when he quit crying. Plus, he'd had those chair legs and he couldn't see a kitchen table with shiny chair legs now without feeling thankful. They didn't have chair legs in Manila, just bad grown-ups and fire.

He moved to the side of the door, but stayed close in case he had to leave quickly. He was there to get warm, to soak up the heat before he had to hit the streets to work the bars.

He didn't want to get noticed, just warm. He moved to the side of the door and leaned back against the wall. Tried to fit in, while he got some of that heat in him.

Moving to the left and staying against the wall put him closer to the old ladies sitting at the table and he realized after a few moments that they were talking to each other in soft whispers.

He could not hear their low-voiced words at first.

Just the sound, an almost-music like a lullaby his

grandmother sang to him when he stayed with her and his hurting knees and elbow bones kept him awake. Her gentle voice-song, crooning. And, just like when he'd been little and his grandmother sang to him, he leaned against the wall and let the sound come over him, which added to the warmth of the library and covered him like a blanket.

He closed his eyes and thought of home, mostly of Edy and Sig. Even though home was something he didn't have, never had. He was only ever in a place. Then another. But a place wasn't a home. And he wished he had more than just places, wished he had a home. Where people waited for him. Like the old ladies sitting at the tables.

The warmth and the light thawed him until at last he could hear their words. Not just as music but as real words. They were talking about their husbands who had passed away – never dead but passed away – and children that had moved away. Husbands had passed and children had grown and everyone else had moved on and they were alone.

So now they came to the library and sat and told their stories to each other in soft voices with the gold light around them because it was cold, deep-northern-killing cold and they couldn't afford to keep their houses warm all through the day and evening.

The fuel oil was too expensive so they turned the heaters down so it wasn't burning so much of their small monthly cheques and they could still afford to buy and make two meat meals a week. But the cold brought them aches and pains so they came to the library where it was warm and they sat and talked and knitted scarves and mittens to give to their children who had moved away. They turned their house heaters down and lived on their memories in the library.

Although he couldn't cry any more, his eyes burned listening to the old women who were soft and gentle with only memories to live on. They didn't complain, they never said anything bad, not even about the oil companies.

That first time he stayed next to the door and listened to the old ladies in their music-talk about their memories, it took him out of himself. Normally he had to think all the time about his own things – what he had to do to get by. Live. How he could live. Where the next food was coming from, the little money he could find or make, where to move, how to stay safe.

Their stories seemed to come alive in him when they talked about how they first came to this country, this northern country. The first thing they remembered was their marriage, and how it had been early on. First saucepan. First plates. First dishes. First cabins with screens on the small windows to keep out bugs. How their husbands had been then. Strong enough to split logs with an axe in one hand. Strong enough to walk behind a horse-drawn plough breaking new soil all day and still laugh at night, singing wedding songs. Bring joy to the house. Bring love.

At first it was like he wasn't there. Part of the wall. Nobody really saw him or thought of him, and the invisibility made him feel wonderfully safe, like he was more than just a kid with a runny nose and bad clothes and a cloth shoulder bag for carrying old newspapers to fake-sell to the drunks. He was part of the wall listening to the old ladies' stories, letting their memories wash over and through him and make him better. If they still saw soft beauty and happiness in their lives, he sure couldn't complain because he took a beating now and then and was forced to move through alleys.

He looked up once when the ladies were talking and he saw the librarian looking at him. Not long and not directly. A sliding glance, her eyes over him and gone. He could tell this was not the first time the librarian had noticed him. He could tell from her look that she'd been watching him listen to the old ladies.

This time, though, he saw her watch him, and when she saw that he had seen her, she gave him a smile. A small one, same as her glance. Sliding look, brief smile and gone. He relaxed against the wall again.

She too was old, but not as old as the ladies at the tables. Maybe forty. That old. But not pushing eighty like he thought the women at the tables might be. Forty with glasses and a little bit of grey in her hair. Small wrinkles at the corners of her eyes that were laugh wrinkles. If not laugh, then at least smile wrinkles. Clear grey eyes glancing over him and gone.

Had they stayed on him, had her eyes caught and held him, he would have left the library and probably never come back. When grown-ups with authority saw you, studied you – even if they smiled and acted nice – it never seemed to work into a good thing. She might have told him to get out, told him he was the wrong kind of person to be there. She could have called the cops and had him taken out of the library because of his bad clothes, his street look, if her eyes held him and locked him down. You never knew. Just never knew with adults.

But she didn't.

Her eyes flicked and were gone and so he felt safe enough to stay. Stayed until nine o'clock, stayed and got warm. Stayed and listened to the old ladies' stories until the library closed and he could go to work at the bars for change and get a grease-bomb hamburger from Elmer – free for a change – and make a dollar seventy-five working the drunk-change gimmick and move back to the basement at the dump – The Dump – and catch some good sleep near the furnace with a belly full of hamburger and money in his pocket.

Good day. Library day.

THE LIBRARIAN

It all blended in. Life. The library. One overlapped the other until it was more a mix than a simple thing. He had run twice before and was caught and brought back by police and religious do-gooders. So when he was gone working the farms he was one thing, one kind of person. And when they caught him and brought him back to what they termed his home – God, he thought, that they could call it a home – he was another kind of person. Alleys, dark streets, working the dam for fish and the bars for change, the basement and his hot plate and cooking pot, setting pins at the bowling alley now and then, and finally, the woods.

When the summer turned to autumn, he spent most of his time in the woods. Too late to run away again with no autumn or winter work on the farms. He had his lemonwood bow and blunt arrows and he hunted and stayed out most of the time. Ate what he could kill. Became pretty good with the bow. Used snares for rabbits and the bow and blunt arrows for grouse. Fishing line for bullheads to vary the meals. Ate sitting or standing by a fire alone, only not alone because he had the woods, like a friend. He knew every sound, every motion, every curve of line and colour. The woods were a close friend.

Now and then, he came into town to get bread. Salt. Cooking lard.

And go to the library.

It happened that way. Somehow, without thinking, the library became part of what he was, what he did. A safe place. Like the woods.

Strangely – considering that it was an official place run by grown-ups – he found himself liking the library. He loved the woods, they were like breathing to him. But he caught himself liking the library. When he couldn't be in the woods – cold autumn rains, deer season when the woods filled with maniac-drunk deer hunters who would shoot at any sound or motion – when he couldn't be there, he would head for the library.

Just slip inside the door and stand to the left. Not talk to anybody. Try to thaw out, maybe even get warm, from the bitter chill outside now that winter was either here or at least on the way. Smell the books and polished wood and later, when the old ladies came, the scent of their lotion – which gave him memory-pictures of his grandmother – and after a time, after many visits just standing and listening, he moved carefully to the magazine rack and looked at magazines.

He did not take them from the rack to a table, didn't even touch them, but stood by them, pretending not to be there, looking out the corner of his eye to see what the librarian was doing at the main desk. She always seemed to be too busy to notice him. He would have gone, if she had really looked at him. Just another grown-up trap then. But she didn't look at him and so he started to look at the magazines.

Sports Afield, Outdoor Life, Boys' Life. Art. Pictures. He was a slow reader and skipped the words unless they were under a picture; stumbled over the words might be a better way to put it. But he saw, learned from what he saw, and found to his surprise that many of the articles about outdoors, about hunting and fishing, were inaccurate. Like the writer really didn't understand what he was trying to say and put down the wrong words. Some artist would do a picture thinking it was right, trying to illustrate what the writer was trying to say, only it was all wrong.

One picture showed a man meeting a bear in the woods, and the bear standing and showing his teeth savage and mean. Didn't happen that way. Bears didn't stand like that. They moved. Slope-shoulder moved in a rolling push and if they didn't like what they saw they either ran away or made a 'wooft' sound to tell you to get out of the way.

He knew because that had happened to him once. The bear didn't hurt him. Just rolled towards him and made that 'wooft' and he just about crapped his trousers. He let the bear move on – like he could do anything else. So he knew that the magazine's showing them the other way, standing and waving their paws around, was wrong.

He thought at first that he should tell somebody.

Maybe tell the librarian. Just a notion and then it was gone. He didn't want to open that door and let her see inside. Not a good fight to try and change things. Better to move on the way the bear did. Shuffle down and roll on by. Make a 'wooft' in your own head.

So, when he wasn't in the woods and had to be in town, he spent time at the library looking at magazines. It wasn't a habit, not really, but something he did without knowing that he was coming to like it. Not realizing that the library had moved into his brain in a strange way, the same as the woods.

He'd start to have a thing in his head, his thinking, a thing he maybe didn't understand or know about – cars or guns or whole countries or stars – and he'd come to the library, to the magazine rack, and try to find the answer to his questions. Try to snag the knowing the way he snagged fish below the dam or snared rabbits in the woods. Snag a kind of knowing out of a magazine.

That's how he'd learned that all stars were suns. Might have planets around them. Might even be a boy like him on one of the planets. That's where he'd learned the woods he loved went all the way north to where there were no more trees and snow, where there was ice almost the year around and people who hunted seals. Or caribou and ate meat raw and what they didn't eat they fed to dogs to pull sleds. That's when he learned to think outside himself about what might come, like how he might some day want to try a sled being pulled by dogs.

The library was how and where and when he came to learn things.

Snag a way to learn out of the library.

Eventually he moved from standing in front of the magazine rack reading to sitting at one of the tables, which only happened because he was hurt, really.

One of the bigger kids who set leagues at the bowling alley was sick and he was offered the chance to work league night. Normal league nights he'd earn seven cents a line, plus tips. Usually, though, there were no tips. Tournament nights, however, meant two alleys, eleven cents a line plus a much better chance of tips, so he took the work for the money even though working two lines at eleven cents a line still meant it took a long time to make two dollars at the bowling alley.

Every alley ended in a wooden pit behind the machine, which had a holding-hole for each pin. After the ball came and knocked the pins down, a pinsetter had to pick up the ball, slam it into the groove track that sent it back to the front to the bowlers, grab the pins and slide them into the holding-holes, heave down on a bar-lever over the machine that put all the pins down and set them right for the next ball that came.

Except if all the pins weren't knocked over – the bowler didn't roll a strike – the boy had to return the ball, grab the pins that did get knocked over, and then get out of the way before the next throw came down the lane. Sometimes, when the bowlers got drunk, they would try to catch the pinsetters in the pit with the ball. Big game, big joke for the big men – hit a kid with the bowling ball. Once a kid nicknamed Cat Eyes, because he swore he could see in the dark, got hit and never got over the limp. Maybe he could see in the dark, but he sure couldn't see the ball coming at him in the light.

But the pits were on the edge of warm, and if you stayed busy, you'd work up a sweat and not feel the cold air coming in the high back window. And you weren't on the freezing streets.

Behind the pits was a narrow wooden bench where the pinsetter could jump, pull his legs up, and hope to be out of the way when the ball crashed into the pins and sent them flying. Two alleys side by side, jump over a small retaining wall between the alleys, pick up the ball, slam the pins into the pin holes, jump back over the wall to the first alley, throw the ball back, set the pins, climb up on the bench out of the way, and then do it all again.

Hard work.

Crippling work.

Dangerous work.

Beer was flowing, and as soon as the bowlers were drunk, they began to throw harder, throw wilder, making bets on whether they could catch the pinsetter in the pit before he could jump out of the way.

The ball was heavy and moving fast. The pins were heavy, flying through the air like bombs going off. If either the ball or a pin caught you, you'd go out like a light and wish to God you hadn't agreed to set pins for the league night.

But you couldn't complain. If you threw a curse up the alley loud enough to be heard, you wouldn't get any tips.

Eleven cents a line. Two lanes going steady. Ten men

bowling three games each. Thirty lines a night. Thirty times eleven – over three dollars. Three dollars and thirty cents for the night of dangerous work.

Plus tips.

Might make five dollars a night when it was added to and shared with other pinsetters. But only if you didn't complain. You'd carry an old pin with you when you left at night to head back to the basement so the big kids wouldn't try to take your money. Had to do it once, take a pin to their heads to protect your earnings, and then they knew. He'd hit a big kid named Kenny with a bowling pin one time – a good full swing with great follow-through – and Kenny went down like he'd been poleaxed. After that, they left him alone and he would disappear in the alleys and be away, his pin money and tip in his pocket, an old pin in his hand, just in case.

There came a day, though, when he moved too slowly. Bowlers were drunk. Lot of bad laughter. Stupid laughter. He worked the pit on the left, then the one on the right, and he had lowered himself down to pick up pins when a drunk bowler, laughing drunk bowler, threw his ball down on purpose to see just how fast a pinsetter could move.

Truth was, he just about made it. Almost cleared the pit but . . . not . . . quite.

He was clear from the pins flying in all directions, but the ball caught him a glancing blow on the left calf just as he pulled his leg up towards the bench. Hurt some, but didn't seem that bad. He was mostly bothered because he'd been caught off guard setting two alleys at the same time. Shouldn't have been caught at all, but he was just clipped, and the ball could have easily broken his leg, could have killed him, catch him in the head and he'd be gone. Happened before. Kid named Curt had been hit in the head and it didn't kill him, but he could never walk or talk right again. Kept saying things over and walked leaning to the side with one eye closed. Might have been better off dead.

So, other than a brief pain jolt, he was lucky that he was all right and he went on setting pins for the rest of the league night. All the while thinking that some day, when he was grown, he would catch the idiot who threw the ball at him and beat the crap out of him. He limped a little after that, not a lot, but enough so it showed when the day got a little long and he would become tired and the leg would ache some.

The entrance to the front of the library had three steps, and when he climbed them after he'd been hit by the drunk bowler, he felt a twinge. As he moved over to the magazine rack, the twinge became more of a nagging pain, so he took an outdoor hunting magazine and sat down at one of the oak tables.

He hadn't been there two, three minutes looking at some art in the magazine showing a man shooting a bow and arrow at an attacking bear – never happen that way – when he felt somebody behind him.

He looked up and saw the librarian.

Standing there smiling at him.

Warm smile.

But she was still a grown-up and she was still noticing him.

She would probably tell him to leave now. Just get out – people like you don't belong here. Drop the warm smile and kick him out.

'Can I help you?'

That was what she said: Can I help you?

He looked up at her. Looked away. Let his eyes fall on the wood of the table. Straight grain. Solid oak. A tiny groove where somebody had scratched the wood with something sharp. Stupid thing to do. He took a breath and thought, Can you help me? God, lady, if you only knew . . .

He shook his head, mumbled something about coming in to get warm. Mumbling worked, seemed to work, when it came to avoiding problems from meeting grown-ups. Adults expected kids to mumble. Act shy, keep looking down, mumble how cold it was outside. Thinking, why did I sit down at the table, looking like I was planning to stay and I got caught. Time to go. Now. How many steps to the door? Four, five, then down the little stairs and out. Away. Not to come back. Not now that she'd noticed him, spoken to him.

But his legs didn't move, his body wouldn't move. He kept his eyes on the table. Waiting. Waiting for her to say it: Get out.

He looked up, a quick glance. Stunned that she was still smiling. Warm smile.

'Can I help you?'

Soft voice. Smiling sound in her voice. Same question. Not saying get out. Offering to help.

Again he shook his head, mumbled something about

getting warm. Lied and said: 'I'm all right.'

But never all right. Sometimes a little more right than others, but never completely right. Every little thing never ever completely all right.

'Would you like a library card?'

And there it was: the hook. The gimmick. There was always that side reason for grown-ups being nice, they always wanted you to do something.

He looked up at her again. She still had that same smile on her face, but now he had it figured out – she was after something from him.

'How much does it cost?'

'The card is free. It doesn't cost anything.'

Right, he thought. I'm thirteen, a hard thirteen, with three years as a kid in the streets of Manila, walking by those awful stains on the wall every day for three years, living the rest of the time in a drunk swamp of a life, or trying to live in it with the vipers, and except for his grandmother giving him pie and rubbing his knees when they hurt, and Edy and Sig giving him a room of his own and jobs of work, nobody had ever given him anything free.

Not a thing.

Ever.

And he thought then that he would leave, should leave. No reason to stay. Not really. But there was her smile and it was warm and it was cold outside and the room was warm and in his brain was this . . . this thing. A smart-aleck-kid thing that made him want to ride this out and see where this was going. See what the gimmick turned out to be. Cocky-kid thinking. Maybe learn the gimmick and then use it against them.

Not sure who 'them' was, or could be, but positive there was a 'them'. Somebody who would use the card against him.

The card.

So he looked up at her again. Longer this time. And then nodded. 'Sure – give me a library card for nothing.'

He had to follow her to the reception, where she had an old, clunky office typewriter and typed his name on a small piece of something like cardboard. Stiff paper. Had a little metal tag in it with a number and he saw she spelled his last name right. Most people ended it '–son', but she typed it '–sen'. The right way. Correct way.

And then she handed him the card.

Didn't say anything, just smiled again as he looked

at the card, held it in his hand, and studied it. His name. His number. And here a strange thing happened. Somehow the card . . . made him real to himself. It was *his* name, *his* number. Right there.

In all the world, he had finally become a real person. Right there. In the world. A real person right *there* . . .

'What do I do with it?'

'You use it.'

'For what?'

'To get books from the library.'

'What books?'

'Anything you want that we have here. Or I can order books from other libraries if you want something we don't have. It might take a week or so to get it mailed here but . . .'

He held up his hand. Not high. They had moved to the desk in front to get his card printed and he just held the hand up a couple of inches off the countertop. But it was still an interruption and went against everything he knew about dealing with grown-ups. You never interrupted them. 'But what does it cost when you actually want to get a book?'

'It's all free. Like I said. Any book you want and it

doesn't cost anything. We are a lending library. You take a book home and read it and bring it back when you're done. One week, two weeks – is the usual time.'

He leaned back, looked at the room, the walls of shelves, shelves built in the middle. All full of books. Thing was, he thought, thing was he hardly ever read very much. He had learned to read, but it wasn't something he spent much time practicing. He couldn't remember actually reading a full book. Oh, some picture books when he was a kid, but not now. Not a whole book with lots of pages. You had to work page to page on those big suckers, had to crank it up, work the pages, one to the next, like a job of work. 'I wouldn't know where to start . . .'

And he realized with a small jolt that he'd said it aloud. Man, he was loading up the mistakes. He'd thought he was thinking, but it came out. Stinking brain took over, didn't it? Talking on its own. Like he was just there watching and his brain was having a talk with the librarian.

'It's a lot of books,' she said with a nod. Still smiling. Warm smile. 'Would you like me to pick one for you to get started?'

He could still have run, could have gotten away clean. And yet he did not go. Did not run. Instead another hot worm came into his brain and he thought: What kind of book could she possibly pick that I could read? Would read? And his curiosity took over the way his brain had taken over and it opened his mouth and he said:

'Sure.'

Just like that. Cocky little bugger. Like he'd been talking to librarians all his life, and she motioned for him to follow her as she led him back into one of the stacks, looked up at the books for a moment, then pulled a book down and handed it to him.

'It's about a boy who lives in the jungle,' she said, 'and what he has to do to survive. I think you might like it.'

But he only half heard her. He was looking at the book, which had a worn cloth backing, rubbed and rounded corners. Didn't open it. Not yet. Felt the corners, the touch of it. Felt warm. The same warm way the librarian smiled. Not a threat. More like an invitation – like the book was almost calling to him. The way her smile pulled him in. Saying come on, follow me. Follow me. He'd seen books before. Of course. But never one that seemed so . . . so alive. Like it wanted to be his friend. Silly thought; how can a book be a friend? But the librarian had done the same thing, said follow me. Into this stack of books.

And for the first time in his life he truly wanted to know this book, know what was in it, how it was, and what he had to do to know what it was saying to him. Really wanted to *know*.

Without thinking or understanding, he pulled the book closer to his chest. 'And I can take this?'

She nodded. In the shade between the shelves and stacks, the light came through in a golden ray, a spray of sun with bits of dust in it that made her face seem to glow. Like the paintings in the churches in Manila. Pictures of a woman bathed in light smiling down on him.

'I need the card from the back of the book so I can print the number of your library card on it and file it by the date it's due to be returned, and then off you go. The normal lending period is two weeks, but if you need more time to finish, you can get an extension.'

And although it was all new to him, this different part of life, in some ways, it seemed familiar. He watched as she turned his card over to copy his number down on the card from the book, then got his library card back and moved out into the streets. He didn't hit the bars to fake-sell papers and slide change from the drunks. Instead, he went into the alleys and worked back to his basement.

Cold outside, so cold it made the hair in his nose crinkle. He had a woollen navy watch cap he'd bought for a quarter at the surplus store that was only a little stained with something that probably wasn't blood, and it kept his ears warm, but he worried about the book. Wondered if the cold would damage it, and if it did, he did not want to go back to the librarian and tell her the book was hurt. Maybe frozen. Could you freeze a book? Break it?

He tucked it inside his jacket and held it against his chest with his arm. Kept it warm. At least a little warm. Not much of a jacket, but it trapped some body heat, maybe enough to protect the book.

It was warm when he got to the basement, and he had a reasonably new loaf of white bread and a jar of peanut butter and a fifteen-cent can of sardines. Made toast and ate a peanut-butter-and-sardine sandwich, drank the leftover sardine juice in the can, sipped a bit of water from the valve in the old wash sink against the wall, and settled into the chair with the book.

His book, *his* book.

From his library card.

His library card.

And he was going to read *his* book, from *his* library card, no matter how long it took.

Read the whole thing.

By God.

BOOKS

Took him almost two weeks.

One hundred and forty-six pages of words to read not counting the extra pages for title and legal mumbo-jumbo. Took him close on two weeks because he was a slow reader. He could read two, three pages at a time, but then he'd forget what happened and he'd have to go back to see what he missed. Read two or three more pages and then flip back to check.

Life went on while he was reading. It was deer season, so he stayed out of the woods while the crazies were out there, shooting at noise and movement, not hunting so much as killing.

Stupid fools would shoot a rabbit or grouse with a deer rifle. Blow small animals like that to smithereens. No meat left. Just shreds. They'd shoot him if he wiggled a bush. Nothing worse than a drunk trying to hunt with a gun too big for him, and a lot of them were so drunk they wound up shooting themselves or other hunters. Every year, eight or ten of them were shot and killed by other hunters.

So he didn't go in the woods for a couple weeks. And this time of the year you couldn't snag below the dam. The fish weren't running until spring, and besides, it was cold. Ice rimmed the river and the temperature stayed below zero. Being near the water made it feel colder and if your hands got wet . . .

Bad news.

So he worked the bars a little more, and Elmer paid him a dollar a day on top of a free grease-bomb burger to sprinkle sawdust on the floor and sweep it up with a broom. Hunters came into the bar every night and worked at their drunks and made a mess, but Elmer didn't mind because they spent money as fast as they could. Mostly the floor job was spit and puke, but every now and then the broom would push up a quarter or two.

A little money.

And he set pins at the bowling alley when it was offered.

A little more money.

Fifty cents a day to clean out the coal clinkers where the boiler in the furnace dumped them. Then check the apartment when the vipers passed out and see what there was in his father's trousers or in his mother's purse.

It all added up, and at the end of each day, he'd sit in his chair by the furnace in the basement and read.

Pretty good book, he thought, but at the same time he wasn't sure if he was capable of knowing whether a book was good or not. He liked it. Sort of. About a boy and his family living on a jungle island in the Pacific Ocean. Caught fish, ate fish cooked in coconut milk, ate rice with their fingers, ate fruit from the trees. Now and then killed a wild pig with a spear and cooked it buried in the ground over hot coals covered with thick leaves.

Green Hope.

That was the title, although he never quite figured out what they might have been hoping for. They had plenty of food, and nobody seemed upset about anything. His parents didn't drink; they were nice to him. The kid swam in a warm ocean and the sharks didn't hit at him.

He read the book.

Read the *whole* book.

And, when at last he was finished, he sat thinking about it. Furnace humming next to him, bright bulb hanging down over him, he closed his eyes and tried to visualize what he'd read, tried to make word-brain pictures from what the writer said about the jungle. About hope.

Thing is, he had spent quite a lot of time in the jungles around Manila when he was a kid and ate fruit from the trees and rice and sardines with his fingers and it wasn't . . . quite . . . the same as the writer seemed to think. He'd written that you swung through the trees when you wanted to pick mangoes, but he knew better. Mangoes fell from the tree when they were ripe and ready to eat. You could walk along and hear them hitting the ground.

Thump.

You didn't have to climb the trees. Just had to get to them on the ground before the other animals did.

Besides, you get up in the trees like you owned them, swinging around grabbing fruit, and the monkeys would bite you. They had teeth like circular saws and they were flat mean. Especially if you were taking their food. He'd never seen a happy monkey, but he'd seen plenty of them that weren't happy. Just snotty mean. Now and then he would see a python that caught a monkey and swallowed it whole. The monkey made a big lump in the snake and he never felt bad about it. You only had to be bitten once to not think much of the monkeys.

Finally, one evening when he had finished the book, he took it back to the library.

He stood inside the door and waited, feeling shy for some reason. The librarian had been talking to some of the old ladies who had started to come again to the oak tables when it got cold and he waited until she was back at the reception.

He handed her the book, set it on the top of the counter, and pushed it across, like an offering.

'Did you like it?' Smile. Same warm smile.

He nodded. He didn't say anything, even though he'd thought he might tell her about what really happened in the jungle. Nothing came out, though, and he just nodded.

'Could you see what the writer was trying to get across?'

He thought about it. Wasn't sure if he really did. Started to nod and instead opened his mouth, but stopped before the words came out.

She waited for him to continue with the same patient smile.

'The words made pictures in my brain. He wrote about jungles and I could see them. I've seen jungles, and when he talked about how green they were, I could see them again in my brain. And the ocean. So blue. And monkeys, but they're mean. And pythons eat them. And mangoes just fall on the ground, you don't need to climb to get them, and then the juice runs down your chin when you bite into them, and there were rotten bodies of dead enemy soldiers in the jungle, the real jungle that I saw, not the one he wrote about . . .'

He wound down. Stopped. Thought, Oh my God, what am I doing? Talking like this to a grown-up. Rattling on like a broken record. And am I doing this? She couldn't know these things, wouldn't possibly understand what

I'm trying to tell her. She probably thinks I'm crazy. I went too far. She'll tell me to leave now.

Instead she nodded. Hesitated for what seemed the longest time to him. Then asked, 'Was all that in the book?'

She was listening. Actually listening to him. He shook his head. 'Not exactly. But the book made me think of things I'd seen when I was a kid in Manila. It was like . . . an opening. Like the book opened my brain to let it see other word-pictures somehow.'

He heard her make a small sound – a soft but sudden breath. And he saw her lower lip quiver a tiny bit and she bit it with her front teeth to stop the quivering. Her eyes misted and he thought, God, she's going to cry. But she didn't. Not quite. Instead she nodded again, and in a soft voice, almost a whisper, she said:

'Isn't that wonderful?'

STORIES

And it went this way:

The first book took a day or so short of two weeks to read. Clumsy, toggling back and forth in the pages to make sure he hadn't missed anything. Brought it back and found out she hadn't lied – didn't charge a thing for it. In fact, she gave him another book.

This one a Western story about a boy training a wild horse that somebody had hurt. The horse became his friend. He liked the book even though he knew nothing of horses, but he still had a bit of a plan to head west and become a cowboy. The horse was black and white, which is called a paint horse. Named

Poncho and ate carrots out of the kid's hand.

Things he hadn't known about horses and now he knew them.

From reading.

He raced through this second book.

One hundred and fifty-two pages.

Knocked that sucker off in a week and one day.

Only had to do skip-back reading a couple of times to check on what he read to not miss anything.

He didn't miss much and he figured that he was getting better at reading. Also realized that he could know more, maybe be more, from reading.

Amazing.

He wanted more, as if he was . . . what? Thirsty. Like his brain was thirsty and wanted more things to know the way he wanted water if he was dry. And not just that he wanted more, but had to have it, like water. That's what came from books, the knowing of new things and then wanting more.

Next book he read in four days, and the fourth book in three days, and then he was reading two books a week, sometimes three. He couldn't get enough of the knowledge-water for his thirsty brain, and there came a time in midwinter when he brought back a history book the librarian had given him – history, for crying out loud – but he had read it all through and learned about Custer getting wiped out at a place called the Little Bighorn River by Cheyenne and Lakota Sioux Native Americans.

The writer had been a bit too real because it brought back brain-pictures of some of the things he had seen in Manila. The kind of things that he had kept in little compartments in his brain so they weren't always there pushing at him.

When he returned the book, she could tell he was a little troubled and she asked what he was thinking. He hadn't meant to, but he found himself telling her about how the book had made some brain-pictures come out of compartments that he didn't always want out in the open. He told her how he'd lived in Manila for three years when he was a kid and had seen things that he hadn't talked about.

'What kind of things?'

'Dust,' he said. 'Heat and dust and noise. Terrible noise. I heard gunfire almost every night in Manila when machine guns would start firing. So fast it was like a giant piece of cloth being ripped. Must have been the same at the Little Bighorn.'

And for a moment he thought she was going to ask another question, push him to talk when he didn't like talking.

But instead she reached under the countertop and brought out a pocket notebook, which she set in front of him. Then she reached down again and came up with a brand-new yellow number-two wooden pencil. She put it in the sharpener and cranked the handle and then set the sharpened pencil on the notebook and looked at him.

'What's this?' he asked.

'It's for you.'

'For school?' He started to suspect a gimmick again – all this was to get him back in school. They kept catching him and making him come back, but he'd wait until they weren't looking and scratch gravel. Be gone. He wasn't going to fall for that just because of a nice smile. No thanks.

'No,' she said, shaking her head. 'It works two ways. You can read and get mind-pictures, which is interesting. And important. But there's the other thing, the other way. You can see things, do things, learn things on your own, and see if you can write them down to make mind-pictures for other people to see. To understand. To know. To know you . . .'

'Who?' Who would ever want to see his private word-pictures? Or understand him or know him – an ugly kid, with bad hair, old clothes, no money. Just nobody. A wrong kid in the wrong place with the wrong people at the wrong time doing all the wrong things. Who would even care about him and what he had to write?

'Who?' he repeated. 'Write it down for who?'

'Well . . .' She hesitated. Looked up at the windows a second. Up into the gold light. Then back down to him. 'Well, me, for instance. You could show it to me.'

Stopped him cold.

And he thought: She's a grown-up.

But she was a grown-up who was nice to him, had a warm smile that she meant, showed him how to feed his brain and understand word-pictures and hadn't asked for a dime from him. Or laughed at him. Or treated him like what he was – street stuff. Or held him off to one side to 'examine' him like so many did.

He turned and left the library without saying a word.

Just turned and left, out into the frigid air and down the alleys to the basement into the old chair by the furnace, and was sitting down before he realized two things.

He had left the library without a book for the first time since he started reading whole books.

And he had taken the notebook and pencil.

The pencil was bright yellow. Like gold. No teeth marks in it. No scuffs. Full-on rubber at one end. She had sharpened it for him, but the point tip had broken off in his pocket. He sharpened it carefully with his small knife, laid it on the arm of the chair. It looked so clean and new, and he thought, It's a present.

She gave me a present.

Then he looked at the notebook. A spiral wire at the end holding it together with a hard blue cardboard cover and a brand name in black ink: SCRIPTO. He lifted the cover and saw the clean white pages with thin blue lines. He counted the lines: fifteen of them. Then the pages: thirty.

He sank back in his chair then, looking at the blank first page.

Which called to him.

Like the page forced him to pick up the pencil and

make a mark on the paper. Make a word. His word.

The paper was waiting. It felt to him like the page was sitting there, like a dare. Come on, smart aleck, write a word. Let's see if you can do it.

He wrote two words: The Deer.

His handwriting sprawled all over the place in dumb big letters. He erased it and rewrote the words in smaller, tighter letters. He controlled the pencil better and got the words down, and he then knew that he would tell the story for her.

He would tell the story of the deer for the librarian.

She was a young doe.

And he had seen her drinking water from the river near where he was camped by the eddy. It was late summer and hot, and the flies were at her and he sat still and watched her stamp her feet, angry at the flies biting her. So graceful and beautiful, but stamping her front feet in a kind of swearing.

And he knew the feeling. Deerflies bit humans as well as deer, other animals. Bit deep and took a little chunk of meat out with the bite and it hurt like blazes and then itched afterward and if you scratched it you bled.

The flies made him mad, too, and he swore when they bit him as well.

They were at her face, working at the corners of her eyes, and she jammed her head down in the water and shook it to get rid of them. But when she raised her head, they were there again in force. Exasperated, she shook her whole front end and dived completely into the water, splashing and slamming her head back and forth, kicking the water in a glorious spray that caught the afternoon sun and made a quick rainbow.

A doe standing in a sudden small rainbow.

He'd held his breath, hoping to make it last, but the moment disappeared as quickly as it formed.

Back on dry ground, she looked at him as if to say, just there, for a moment, the flies didn't bother me. And, in that glance, he knew her. Before she turned and leaped away, still trailing the flies, he knew her not as a deer but as another person. A friend.

A friend to be met in the woods. And he closed his eyes, trying to remember everything about her. How she looked, how she moved, the marks on her so he would know if he saw her again, when he saw her again.

And he did.

Only she was dead. After deer season, he was back in the woods, moving through the trees in fresh snow, and he came upon her lying on her side. One of the idiotic drunk deer hunters had shot her poorly, hit in the gut, and she had run and the hunter had let her go without even trying to find her and end it clean, and she had crawled into some willows and died.

Where he found her and knew it was her because he had memorized everything about her, every mark, every lay of her coat, and now she was ended. His friend. Snow in her eyes, red blood spreading and frozen from the wound in a spray, a hideous red rainbow in the snow. And he thought, Oh God, why did she have to die this way? There was not a word for how he felt looking at her. Not sad. But more. Hurt deep inside as if he had been shot himself.

He had seen many dead things.

Sometimes, when he used to sell papers in the hospital before he worked the drunks in the bar, he would come upon people who had just died. He knew by the copper smell, the copper-alcohol smell and the flat white light. He'd seen dead people in Manila after the machine guns were through. Broken and fallen people, like posed, busted puppets when the string snapped, wild chickens pecking at the bodies.

But they were not . . . what? Not graceful as the doe had been. Who had been forced to crawl into the willows to hide and die alone after some drunk deer hunter gut-shot her and left her.

To say he was sad wasn't even close.

Small tears. He cried alone there kneeling in the snow with her body and tried to remember everything little about her when she was alive so he could remember her that way. Alive. In the river shaking the flies off. The look she gave him.

And later, a year later, sitting in the basement with his notebook and yellow pencil gifts, he wrote the story of the deer for the librarian with a warm smile, and he tried to not leave anything out, but wrote of how the doe had been alive and when he found her dead and the bodies in Manila . . .

He wrote all the word-pictures as well as he could, and still later he wrote of setting pins and working on farms and even later he wrote about how he lied about his age and joined the army and he wrote of marriages and unmarriages and becoming a sergeant and wrote of that, too.

He wrote all of that.

He wrote everything he could remember.

He wrote for the librarian with the warm smile. Even after she was gone and he was living in new places, living new ways, even then he carried the notebook with a blue cover and a yellow pencil and wrote all he saw and did and could remember.

Always for the librarian with the warm smile.

Who first showed him how to read the whole book.

Part V

SOLDIER

1957

He was not exactly certain when it appeared to him that the military was any kind of a solution to his problems. The decision defied sensible reasoning, which at best was convoluted and at worst – which was the norm; it seemed for a long time that all his reasoning turned out to be the worst – incredibly tangled. He knew what the military was like. He had known soldiers in Manila. How they lived or, in some cases, didn't live. And he had no illusions about the life of a soldier. A person only had to see dead soldiers rotting in a jungle one time for that to happen. And yet . . .

And yet, somehow, the thought of the army came to mind.

Started like this: He had been thirteen and everything changed when he found books.

And then he was fourteen and headed out west to work on farms, or become a cowboy and make his fortune. That's how his mind worked when he was fourteen: Head out to make his fortune.

He'd earn two, three dollars a day, eat stale food off a metal pie plate nailed to a board, sleep on gunny sacks in a shed, drink water out of a hand pump. If he was lucky. At the end of summer, he'd go back to town, but really back to the woods and working the bars and living in the basement of the apartment building next to the furnace. Warm, but shared with rats.

Then he was fifteen and headed back out west, more west, further west, West, and four dollars a day this time. One part of the summer working in a fresh-frozen Bird's Eye vegetable factory for a dollar an hour. Pulling boxes of corn, peas, string beans off the conveyor as they came shooting out of the machines ten at a time, pull ten over to the freezer tray, ten more, ten more, push the tray down to the freezer and ten more, ten more . . .

Huge eight dollars a day. Twenty-eight minutes for lunch from a vending machine. Puke-tasting can of chili eaten with a tiny wooden spoon. Globules of unmelted orange fat and slimy beans that took most of his daily pay and had him crapping like a goose, crap so hot it seemed to make his rear end steam, and then sleep in the brush in clouds of mosquitoes not far from the factory.

Then he was sixteen and back out west still again to work farms or ranches or become a cowboy and have a horse and ride the range except that, this time, he took a job with a carnival troop and learned about life, no, Life, from a woman named Wanda.

But before that, even before going west again and again and the woods, came the school problems. It didn't work for him; school, the concepts of studying and making friends, the playing nicely with others and doing his work on time, simply did not function for him. Square-peg–round-hole kind of thing.

In time, his problems went still further, became antagonistic. He'd run and they'd come after him, with the law at times, trying harder and harder to get him to be something he felt he could never be, force him to fit in.

Fit the heck *in*.

Mash the square peg hard enough and it would eventually fit impossibly in that round hole. The cops would take him to school, drag him into the building, turn him over to the system that would start mashing him into the wrong hole shape.

He had seen, been, done too much. Thought: What do you talk about? Clothes? Girls? Sports? He shuddered to think of even trying to play those games. He never had the right clothes and wouldn't have known how to wear them if he owned them. He'd roamed the dark streets of Manila hundreds and hundreds of nights where there were soldiers and night women, and he'd seen and heard them too many times to feel anything akin to romance when he was with school girls. He thought all sports were silly: You see a kid run to a fence and try to climb it to raid a soldiers' camp just so he has something to eat and he gets cut in half right there in front of God and the world by machine-gun fire, and basketball seems inane.

Perhaps, he thought, that was when he began to think the only place for him was in the military.

But before that, when school became a burden, and then an overburden, he simply ran. Got out. Rewrote his grandmother's philosophy: If it sucks Here, go over There.

He'd head for the woods because, if he stayed in town, they would sometimes find him, bring him back, say strong things to him. But, in the end, it didn't work. In the end, it was just that, the end.

When he looked ahead in his life, he didn't see anything to do with school. Only work and trying to make it through each day alive and, of course, the woods.

The library was always there and books, still more books, and by the time he was full-on sixteen he was reading like a wolf eats. Devouring books, learning to know, but that only took him further from school.

The librarian guided him, gently, with kindness, into new kinds of books and she started to get him to read history. In particular, he read a book about Napoleon and his soldiers and their insane, abortive attempt to invade Russia, which nearly wiped out the whole army as thousands of men starved and many more froze to death in the unbelievably cold Russian winters.

Turns out that his history class in school was studying Napoleon at the same time, and the teacher – who was really the football coach pretending to be a teacher, thick neck, small brain – was lecturing about Napoleon in Egypt and called on the boy to tell what hardships they had suffered. The boy, who had been reading about the winter campaign in Russia and misunderstood the question – which was slightly mumbled – replied that the number one problem was troops freezing to death.

The teacher brutally pointed out his mistake: You didn't freeze to death in Egypt. He made a point of teasing the boy until he had the whole class laughing at him. Stupid boy – freezing troops in Egypt – how dumb could you be? The boy was always teetering on the edge of complete social disappearance anyway, and the teasing pushed him still further apart in school, away from any kind of social acceptance.

And so the woods. The library and the librarian were his friends, where he would go to know more, be more, and the woods became his living room, his place to live. And school, all that went with school, was the grey, dead thing that threatened to take away his . . . his everything.

Then came sixteen.

He went out west again, but he was a little too early and he couldn't find farmwork because the fields were too wet to work. He had a little money and he lived in an old abandoned building on the edge of a small town waiting for a job to open up. Sardines and crackers, twice a day. Sixty cents a day for food. Water free from an old hand pump in a nearby vacant lot.

He was near done after a few weeks of living rough and on the edge of heading back to the woods for the summer, when a county fair came to town and he went out to see if there was a chance of getting some work. He picked up a job helping put up rides for five dollars a day and the man who owned the Tilt-A-Whirl, name of Tucker, hired him on for the summer.

Five dollars a day. Thirty-five dollars a week. He couldn't believe how much money he'd make. A hundred and forty dollars a month. Even if he spent some change on day-old hot dogs and tired sloppy-joe sandwiches from the snack wagon, he'd make more than if he'd been working ranches or farms for three dollars a day. He'd be rich. He didn't mind sleeping across the truck seat at night. And Tucker showed him how to work the clutch on the Tilt-A-Whirl to suck change out of the pockets of the hicks wearing loose pocket dungarees. Hicks were even better targets than the drunks in the Northern Lights saloon in terms of taking their money.

Easier money and less chance of taking a thump like he did if the drunks saw him scraping change for himself, since the hicks were most of the time busy puking their guts up after the ride. Might be another two or three dollars a day on top of the five.

Just making good hard money.

And then there was Wanda, who was Tucker's wife, and blond and old, but not that old, who was a dancer in a sideshow where she showed the hicks her body a little at a time. More than once, the boy – who was a hick himself – had snuck in for a peek.

But then Tucker caught one of his carnival workers with Wanda, and he was a little drunk and they had a knife fight, and the cops came and there he was, the boy, a runaway, a Runaway, and wham, he was detained. Not arrested, but picked up by the cops and sent back home again and, wham, back in school again, so not arrested, but in jail anyway.

At least until he could split ass and make it into the woods, at least until everybody stopped watching him, took their eyes off his business for more than a minute and he could run again.

Except now he was reading all the time because of

what he had learned from the library and librarian, and so he knew things. Knew some things. Most important that he could be more, do more, become more some day. He didn't want to be some bust-ass grunt labourer the rest of his life and then, right then, the government stepped in.

The state got sick of chasing after him skipping school and always running away, so they took over and sent him to some social worker/counsellor/do-gooder. He was told he had to go or else get sent to a 'home' where you were detained even worse than when he'd been detained but not arrested working for Tucker and sent back to school. They called the place the Murphy Home for Boys and promised that they'd lock your ass in every night.

The counsellor sat him down in a room across a grey table and gave him a cup of coffee so stiff it would hold a spoon upright, leaned back in his chair, lit a cigarette with yellow nicotine-stained fingers, and said: 'You're pretty much pissing your life away.'

The boy didn't say anything. Just sat.

'Do you want to change that?'

What do you want me to do? the boy thought.

Find Jesus? Go to school and find Jesus? Go to school and become a nice kid living in a nice family and find Jesus? Or did he have some other fairy tale in mind? Maybe find a lamp and rub it and get three wishes and then find Jesus? Come on. The man across the table was as thick as an oak board. The boy smiled to himself, thinking, You could saw him up and make a library table out of his butt.

He still didn't say anything, because this man had nothing to offer. He'd sit there, wait out the wood man, leave as soon as he could, and head out. Split. Like always.

'So . . .' The counsellor took a long drag on his cigarette and the boy wondered whether he should start smoking. Looked cool. Smoking might make him look older so he could pass . . . for what? Pass for somebody who looked older. Another drag on the cigarette. L.S./ M.F.T., like the radio commercials said, Lucky Strike Means Fine Tobacco. Even sounded cool.

'So, since the way it's going, you're going to flunk out of school, the state has this new programme they're starting for people who have trouble with regular school. They call it vocational training school. That way you can learn a trade even if conventional school doesn't fit you. There are two versions – you can either become an automobile mechanic or a television repair man. You pick. The school will pass you into the twelfth grade, and instead of going to normal school, you will attend one of the two vocational schools five days a week. You miss three days running and you're out and into the Murphy Home.'

And it was that moment that changed him. Changed everything.

He had made friends with a boy named Leo who had been a ham radio enthusiast, and the boy found himself enjoying everything about being a ham operator. Leo had a small thirty-watt transmitter hooked to a dipole antenna outside his room, and he helped the boy make a small oscillator out of spare parts, which aided him in learning Morse code. The two of them would sit for hours when the skip signal was working, and talk in code to people all over the world. Sometimes even as far away as Russia, where it was forbidden to have a radio, let alone communicate with people in other countries . . . if you considered it communicating to ask and answer the same question over and over again: Where are you?

The boy had thought that if he ever found a place to settle down, he would get his amateur licence and work the network. In the meantime, he visited Leo and learned as much as he could about amateur radio. And electronics. And television, which was just entering the public world then, and seemed a strange and magical thing – that you could shoot a beam of electrons through space and get a picture, a motion picture on a screen, didn't seem possible.

And this man, with the nicotine-stained fingers and yellow teeth, was offering him a chance to learn about television. And electronics. How they worked. How they made things happen that seemed magical.

'I want,' the boy said, 'to become a television repair man.'

'With the aforementioned restrictions?'

Nobody, the boy thought, uses words like 'afore-mentioned restrictions' with a straight face. But the man wasn't smiling.

The boy nodded. 'Sure.'

'Three days and you're out.'

Another nod. 'Sure.'

And it was done. Just the way the man said. When

he was about to flunk out of the eleventh grade, the state stepped in and he was passed to twelfth grade with the 'proviso' (their word, not his) that he was to pay attention and really try to learn a vocation as a television repair man and not be a 'burden to society'. Again, their words. He didn't want to have anything to do with society, even as a burden. So he kept nodding and smiling and learning everything he could about Ohm's law and how vacuum tubes (this was well before transistors and silicon controlled rectifiers) functioned and exactly how television worked. And even then, when he knew and understood it, the whole thing still and always seemed magical to him. Take a picture of a person, break the picture down, shoot it through space on a radio beam to another place, and rebuild the person.

Pure magic.

And he loved it. Ate it with a spoon, ravenous to know more and more, to figure out how it all worked and to really *know* everything there was to learn about this new thing. And although he did not even sense it at the time, he would find later that the knowledge, the technical base of the knowledge, would affect him profoundly and for the rest of his life.

In the meantime, however, regular life went on. He still had to earn enough money to live, and he added trapping to his normal workload of working the bars and setting pins – mostly for leagues, now that he was older. He set small snare lines and trapped some mink, now and then a raccoon, a couple of fox, and sold rabbits for a dime, and later a quarter each, to mink farmers for domestic mink food.

All this hard work added hours to each of his days, in addition to his time at school. But he never missed a day of classes, even though he set the line and checked it each morning, and set pins or cleaned the bar every night.

He never got ahead. He could never quite catch up with all he had to do each day, and every night, after the long hard days, he'd fall into his easy chair in the basement or crawl in the back seat of the car in a dead stupor.

Add to this the newfound interest in girls, which he did not fully understand since all he knew was what little he'd glimpsed of Wanda at the carnival, and that certainly didn't help him fit in well with high school girls. He finally worked up enough courage to ask a girl out on a date, but she looked him up and down, said: 'With you?' followed by a smirk and a short laugh, and that was that. He felt some relief since he couldn't have afforded much of a date anyway.

He never seemed to have enough time. He had dropped back into the world, his old world, where he needed alleys and the library to stay safe from the bigger kids who were bullies. Between school and having to keep up a hustle morning and night, he didn't have time to pay attention to his safety the way he should have, and there came a day when they caught him cold out in the open as he was crossing the railroad yards heading for the woods to check snares.

Big kid named Benny cornered him by one of the equipment sheds. Took a swing at the boy, which he ducked and took on his shoulder. Took another swing. Or started one.

Only this time things were different.

Very different.

The boy had grown stronger, tougher, quicker. And, in some ways, meaner.

He had an edge now.

Some of the men he'd worked with in the carnival

were from the other part of living; they'd done time in prison where they had to know how to fight, and they'd brought this knowledge to the carnival. The boy not only started to comb his hair in a ducktail, cut the belt loops off his Levi's, wear a pair of engineer boots, but he knew how to think like, act like, the men from the carnival now.

The carnival men would drink a few beers, take a sip or two of whiskey, and so, of course, fighting was the next thing, the natural thing, in the evenings after the carnival shut down. But one of them, a skinny, runty man with hardly any teeth and crude prison tattoos, Billy, seemed to skate right through the middle of the booze and anger without ever fighting. Men might drink a couple of beers, sip some whiskey, and look Billy's way. But he'd make a sound, an animal snarl, and nobody touched him. They might have thought about making a move on him, but one glance at his face after he made that sound, and everyone backed off, left Billy alone. Only made a move on Billy one time, never a second try to get him to take a swing.

One day the boy was holding the pegs while Billy drove steel car axles into the ground with a twelve-pound sledgehammer so they could help Tucker set up the sideshow tent. Billy never missed, never hit the boy's hand with the sledge. The boy was careful and timed it right and jerked his hand away just as the hammer slammed into the axle but, still, easy enough to miss and bring that sledge down wrong.

He was studying the tattoos on Billy's arms as the hammer came down. Blue snakes on each arm wrapped around a naked woman. Snakes seemed to move, tighten their coils with the movement of the muscles under the skin, looked powerful and very fast, and he looked into Billy's face and said: 'How come you never fight?'

Kind of a snoopy question, and for a breath, then two, Billy looked off into space. The boy wasn't sure he would answer and thought, God, I hope I didn't piss him off. Then Billy shrugged, stretched his arms – quick coiling and relaxing of the blue snakes around the women – and said: 'I don't have to fight.'

The boy thought he might as well go whole hog. 'How come?'

This time Billy shrugged. 'Something I learned in prison.'

The boy waited.

'I'm small. Was small. People, men, tried to work me. Take me. Use me. Steal from me. I made them stop.'

The boy nodded. 'I've seen that. They'll start to come at you, and then change their minds. Why is that? Why do they back off?'

'It's in my eyes. The secret.' He looked out again, away from the boy, maybe back in time.

'What secret?' The boy thought of the mean bigger kids and how they made him run to safety. Forced him to hide and move in the alleys in the dark. If there was a way . . .

'It's not too hard to figure it out' – Billy half smiled, showed a hole where a tooth was gone – 'you've got to be ready to hurt someone. No matter what they do to you, while they're pounding on you, you've got to be ready, got to be absolutely willing, to hurt some part of them. Bite a nose off, tear an ear loose, kick their gonads into next Saturday. Really bring a hurt down on them and the next time they want to mess with you, they'll remember what it was, how it felt, and they'll back off. Pretty soon, it shows in your eyes. Shows that you will do it no matter what comes and even the ones you never fought before will drift, will back away before it starts. It's like they can smell it. Smell that you're dangerous.'

He learned that. The boy had worked the farms hard from morning until dark, slept hard, ate hard, and in the end, turned hard. Like leather that's been cured tough so that his skin felt dense, muscles coiled under thick skin, and on top of the hardening, he absorbed all that Billy told him coming from perhaps the hardest place in the world, prison.

The boy that Benny cornered in the railroad equipment buildings wasn't quite a boy, and while he hadn't become what he would some day become, he wasn't frightened any longer.

He was, had become, whipcord tough. Tied tight inside like a pressured spring about to explode, and though Benny couldn't see it, the boy had become a dangerous thing, somebody you didn't want to corner in an equipment shed.

Without thinking – he had, indeed, no plan – the boy caught Benny by the belt and the collar of his shirt, flipped him in the air and down on his back and brought his knee down on Benny's chest.

Hard.

Heard air come out of both ends.

Benny's eyes shut tight, then opened like saucers while he tried in vain to get some breath. Any breath. Surprised both of them and made the boy smile down on Benny's face.

Not even mad. Just something that had to be handled. Like a good, bad dog. Thought he might bite, but changed his mind.

'No more, right?' The boy said it quietly, but when Benny didn't nod at once, he brought the knee down hard again. Pushed the words a little harder with the knee. 'No more.'

This time Benny nodded, still trying to find breath, and the boy stood back and turned from him and walked away, leaving Benny on his back gasping. Didn't even look back.

Looked forward. Tried to understand what happened. What changed. No. What needed to change, now that he was different, was not the same boy. Was somehow not a boy at all any more. Was becoming something else, changing into something else.

Not a man yet. Though he had hope. Sixteen, near seventeen, but still thinking boy thoughts. And yet he knew the other thing was coming, that he had to be ready for it. Ready to stop thinking of small things and focus on the larger picture. Get prepared. Learn to grow the hell up.

And that's when the idea solidified:

The army.

RA27378338

He decided that the sergeant who met the train at the depot in Colorado Springs wasn't quite human. Nor was he alone. With him were two corporals and one private first class, and all four of them, Sergeant Grim, Corporals Fitz and Jackson, and Private First Class Yello, were also not quite human.

All of them, it seemed, were cut from the same cloth. The fabric of which made them appear – the boy had trouble coming to an identification – 'impervious'. That was the word. They seemed to be structured from some material that made them immune to anything even remotely human, from feeling pain, joy, affection, pathos.

Tough beyond recognition, like stone, they ordered the new men who were still dressed in civilian clothing from the train with brutally loud and surgically cut, short and profane commands.

'No talking!'

'Get off the train, maggots!'

'Stand in a row, maggots!'

'Say "here, sir" when you hear your name, maggots!'

It was late September and 2 a.m. on a cold morning when the train from Fargo, North Dakota, arrived in Colorado Springs. There were forty men on the train, perhaps half of them two-year draftees who most emphatically did not want to be there, and the other half, like the boy, enlistees who had signed up for three years. They had been asleep in their seats when the train arrived, and many of them had not had time to use the bathroom before being ordered off. They were ordered, nonetheless, to stand in ranks while the roll call was finished, and when it was found that one man was missing, the two corporals went back on the train, found him still asleep, grabbed him, and dragged him, kicking and swearing, out of the train and threw him into position with the other men.

They were then ordered to do a right face – about a third of them turned left and had to be corrected, which involved swearing and dealing out pain – and then they were walk-marched to and jammed in olive-drab buses for the short trip to Fort Carson, Colorado.

He had been in the army six days.

Until then it had been simple enough. They graduated him from high school, considering the vocational school segment as a wide kind of credit, handed him a diploma – his parents weren't there and nobody cared about him or applauded him – and, aside from becoming adept at electronics and able to troubleshoot and repair television sets, school had meant nothing to him.

He had just turned seventeen and could legally enlist in the army if he had his parents' permission. He went from graduation to the recruiting sergeant the next morning after forging his father's signature on a permission form, swore himself in, was then told to report to the train depot in Fargo to take the train to Colorado two days later.

At the train depot there were twenty-six men waiting for transport to Fort Carson. Roughly half of them were young enlisted men and the other half, older draftees.

The young men were, for the large part, enthusiastic and eager to be in the military; the draftees were, to a man, furious they had to be there. Some of them – perhaps because they had angered their draft boards, or were outright criminals and allowed to be drafted rather than go to prison – were downright mutinous.

In a moment of what could only be called absurd error, the recruiter had put the boy in charge of these men. The boy had objected, but the recruiter said since he had a military background – he knew of the boy's time in Manila and that his father had been an officer – he was a natural for the job. And besides, it was only for the overnight train ride to Colorado. All he had to do was keep track of their papers and orders. What could go wrong?

But the normally overnight train ride took three days and two nights. Due to a scheduling error, the car was disconnected and held over on a siding in the Omaha stockyards for a day and a half. They were fed stale meals made of semi-mouldy bread and colourfully tainted baloney coated with green mustard. Initially, the men threw the sandwiches away, but in the end, hunger became overwhelming, and they ate them in spite of their appearance. The smell was so thick from the hundreds of cattle being held for shipment on both sides of the tracks that the food tasted like cow dung anyway.

On the second day, the situation became critical as the men – particularly those who had been drafted against their will – rose up in anger and threatened to run away from the train car, and the boy-not-yet-a-man had great difficulty trying to keep them together. There was nobody he could contact, and the only inhabited building nearby was a grubby stockyard bar with what looked like a dead body lying in front of it. It was called, in broken letters crudely painted on a grey board, THE LOADING CHUTE, and when one of the draftees made a break for it and went into the bar, he was – literally – thrown clear of the front door and was very grateful to get back to the railcar in one piece.

With twenty-some-odd men eating the scattered remnants of the horrific box lunches they had been provided, the toilet on the end of the car soon filled up, heaped over – adding to the foul stench of the cattle. In the end, the only thing that kept them together was the fact that the boy-not-yet-man held their orders in manila envelopes as paper hostages. They could be charged and arrested if they didn't have access to and control of their papers. To run from the army, which they were now legally a part of, was a felony and they had been warned they would spend at least two years in Leavenworth Federal Penitentiary.

And besides, they were in the middle of a stinking sea of knee-deep cow dung, and there was simply no place they could run to.

When the mistake was at last realized, late on the third day after two nights, they were hooked to a passenger train and – treated like lepers and forbidden to leave the car they were in lest it make the other passengers ill – taken nonstop to Colorado Springs where they arrived at two in the morning stinking, roiling, in the thick and cloying odour of excrement and vomit, and aching with a driven thirst and starving hunger.

To be greeted by the sergeant and cadre who were not quite human.

Welcome, the boy thought, to The Army.

The procedure for incoming recruits, which was never seen by nor understood by civilians, was to systematically attempt to destroy every vestige of their previous civilian status and life, and rebuild it with military thinking, living, existing.

And although it fit well into what the boy wanted done to his life – cancel out all the crap, change everything – it was, in many ways, brutal.

After the short bus ride to Fort Carson, they were pushed into one of the older wooden barracks filled with sixty bunks made of wire springs and bare tick mattresses at four in the morning.

All the men fell on the mattresses and slipped into unconsciousness, fully clothed and still stinking, only to be jerked awake two hours later by Yello banging a glass Coke bottle around the inside of an empty metal rubbish bin. He ordered those who could get on their feet to physically drag those who could not wake up off their bunks and out the door to stand in formation in front of the barracks.

After something resembling a roll call – some were still virtually asleep on their feet, or leaning against each other – they were pushed (marched would be too orderly a word) to a small mess hall. There they were given a spoon one man said was as big as a shovel, a dollop of powdered eggs on a metal tray, a half cup of something watery and brown that only a deluded optimist could call applesauce, two pieces of dry toast, and a fibre cup of pitch-black coffee, of which they had four and a half minutes to eat and drink. All the while, the cadre stood over them explaining it was a crime to waste food in the army, and if the tray was not scraped with the spoon and then wiped with the toast so that all remnants were eaten, everything would then have to be licked clean. Two men – draftees – didn't believe it and had their faces shoved down on their trays until they were licked spotless. They had brown stains on their faces all day from the applesauce.

Then outside, and more push-walking to begin the destruction-and-rebuilding phase of what Sergeant Grim told them was their 'army career'.

First to wooden supply barracks, which had been turned into a storage shed. Civilian clothes off, including underwear, and stuffed into paper bags with their names crudely lettered on the side, along with their serial numbers, and then, naked, into a cold shower where they were sprayed down. Then another supply shack where they were provided uniform clothing, stacked arm-over-head high, and given two minutes to get into underwear and fatigues – all massively too large. After they showered and dressed, they were herded into yet another building filled with heavy black combat boots that they had another two minutes to put on over heavy olive-drab woollen socks.

And then, and then, and then . . .

Run everywhere. Not jog, but run, and if you fell down or fell out, you were told to give a hundred push-ups or a hundred sit-ups right there in the dirt with cadre screaming into your ear, and when – not if, but when – you failed, the penalty was to be given another hundred push-ups.

Run to another building where barbers cut the hair down to bare skin, before out at a run to yet another building where a man with a wooden tongue depressor checked first your mouth and teeth and tongue and – same wooden tongue depressor – your penis and scrotum.

To see if you had any sexually transmitted disease or crabs. If you had venereal disease as a soldier, you would be charged with 'destruction of government property' and sent to prison.

Now a blind staggering run to the next building, where medics were waiting with hypodermic needles for vaccinations, both arms. Back outside to run back to another building for a blanket, two sheets, a pillow, and a pillowcase. Another run to the barracks to make your bed, two minutes, hospital corners on sheet and woollen blanket with a big US to be exactly in the centre of the bed. Run to the mess hall for a sloppy joe burger that one man swore tasted like fried cat, with four (count them) burnt french fried potatoes that tasted as if they had been violated by rancid lard, and more of the dark watery applesauce for dessert and the ubiquitous black coffee, all of which must be eaten and drunk in four minutes, scraped or licked clean. More running back outside, standing in formation to run to their first class: Soldier Etiquette. Sitting on the ground in the dirt while a corporal drew pictures on a chalkboard on how to stand at attention – fingers on the outside seams of your fatigue trousers, neck and chin stiff and braced. How to salute and prove you understood which was your right hand and which one was your left. Had to hold them and demonstrate: 'This is my right. This is my left.' And if, because of entirely logical exhaustion, you fell asleep – several men toppled over into the dirt completely out – you had to get up and run around the group of men in the dirt to keep you awake while learning the mysteries of soldier etiquette.

Running, for most of them, was a nightmare. Some of the draftees were from New York City, which was perhaps twenty feet above sea level. Fort Carson, in the foothills of the Rocky Mountains, was on the order of six thousand feet above sea level. For somebody from a much lower altitude, the air was almost too thin to breathe. Pity did not exist from the staggeringly tough and well-shaped cadre who would run next to a recruit facing *backwards* and bellowing commands. It verged on the impossible for the eastern recruits and still they had to run.

And run.

Coupled with the forced running everywhere, to make it worse, they had to wear full-on, high-top, thick-soled, stiff leather heavy combat boots while they ran. Each boot weighed over a pound, making the recruits, now running on blisters, clomp along like Frankenstein monsters. Men dropped like flies, falling next to the road unconscious, some bleeding from their mouth, a mixture of snot and blood out of their nostrils. Nor were they left to lie. Other recruits had to pick them up and carry-drag them along at a run to the next place, to the mess hall at four o'clock, eating elbow noodles with a sauce made largely of ketchup, with black coffee and two pieces of dry bread.

At the end of the day, back to the barracks.

Home.

To crash on their bunks fully clothed. Several got no further than collapsing inside the door, passed out on the floor. But nearly everyone felt like they were dying, falling into some coma-like sleep, where they were.

Having had a more physical life, working on farms and setting pins, hunting and fishing in the woods, the boy made it to his bunk and closed his eyes. Around him, he heard some men sobbing quietly in the darkness and at least one asking for his mother.

Day one of so-called active duty in the United States Army.

Four the next morning up with slam-rattling Coke bottle in the rubbish bin, four minutes to dress, four more to finish ablutions, then meet on company street in fatigues and heavy combat boots for the first one-mile run. In a week, it would be increased to two miles and, in another week, to three. But now, on day two, it was a one-mile stagger for most of them. Hacking, blowing snot, wheezing, not even having enough strength to swear, cadre trotting backwards next to them, heading to the mess hall.

More powdered eggs, with fried potatoes on top, black applesauce, and two pieces of toast with – a treasure – a pat of butter.

Food wolfed down in four minutes. Gulp down the coffee. Then outside in formation to run to a field to undergo an hour of callisthenics – a series of jumps, squats, push-ups, sit-ups, overlapping one to the next after which, impossible by now to believe, a break.

A full ten minutes to sit on the ground. Lie back in morning sun. Think of nothing. Cry.

Then up to run to the next class, history and something called a 'mission statement', sitting cross-legged in the dirt.

Awake.

Wake up, awake, maggots!

Drone from the instructor, an officer, a young second lieutenant, really not much older than the recruits.

'During the Second World War and Korea, it was found that only five per cent of infantry soldiers actually fired their rifles at the enemy.' The officer spoke in a monotone that one wag later said was more deadening than anaesthetic. 'You are the first evolution to undergo a new army training procedure known as Trainfire. You will use the same rifle – the M-1 Garand, a thirty-calibre gas-operated semi-automatic shoulder weapon – but where they used to fire at circular bullseye targets, once your rifles are zeroed, you men will fire only at darkened human silhouettes, which will spin and fall if they are hit.'

Most of these men, the boy thought, had never even seen a rifle, let alone fired one. The boy had seen hundreds. This one in front of him was the same rifle the soldiers in Manila had used. Fired the same cartridge used in the machine guns. The ground was covered with literally thousands of fired empty .30-calibre cartridge cases. Wherever you kicked you would kick up a spray of brass cases. And he had seen them fired. At people.

Class over, run to another field, one hour of something euphemistically called close-order drill. Marching – again, staggering – learning left from right in case they had forgotten, which some apparently had, and more marching back and forth, physically jammed into formation when they strayed, and, when it was done, run . . .

Run.

Back to the mess hall for noon chow, grilled cheese on toast and tomato soup with unidentified chunks floating in it, dark watery applesauce (more now, a full cup) for dessert and – another treasure – not black coffee, but weakly flavoured sugared lime water in a fibre cup. Everything eaten or drunk in four or five minutes. They'd say, 'take ten minutes, but expect five, and you might get two.'

Then run back to the field for more close-order-drill stagger-marching, then run back to yet another building where – wonder of wonders – they were made to file in, sit at desks, and begin army aptitude testing.

Question: If all horses are dogs and no dogs are fish, can any fish be horses?

Question: If a train moving sixty miles an hour is sixty miles from Cleveland, how long will it take to reach Cleveland?

Question: How does a radio work?

Question: What is the purpose of Ohm's law?

The answers are to determine if the recruit thinks

mathematically and will fit into the spanking-new technical army that used missiles and radar and computers and nuclear warheads to kill people along with rifles and bayonets.

And because of his television-repair classes and working with ham radio, the boy passed the technical tests with flying colours.

'You are,' said the second lieutenant supervising the tests to the boy, 'the new high-tech army's wet dream. Almost certainly you will be sent to further, advanced-technical schooling.'

But first . . .

Ahh, yes. In the army there is always a 'but first'.

But first he must learn to march correctly and stand correctly and kill properly with a rifle and a bayonet and a hand grenade and piano wire and a knife and a hand axe and a flamethrower and a mortar and an artillery explosion and a machine gun and a recoilless rifle and a bazooka and even a shovel, for God's sake, slash the shovel across the back of the neck with the sharp side-edge.

And over the next weeks and months, the boy learned these things and became so good at them he was made a squad leader and awarded a medal that said: EXPERT.

He became expert at knowing how to kill, seeing the dark figure of a man spin and fall when he fired his rifle.

Spin and fall.

Never saw that in Manila. Saw them double up in a spray of red mist as bullets hit them. Saw them blown backwards when hit by a heavy burst of machine-gun fire. Saw them simply come apart and drop like old meat when they were chopped by bullets.

Never saw them spin and fall.

He was different when, at last, he finished initial combat training. He knew that he had changed and was not and would never again be what he had been in the town where he set pins and dodged bullies and found a measure of sanity and sanctuary in the library.

But he was not yet what he would become.

SPIN AND FALL

They sent the boy to school after school after school in the army. Nike Ajax antiaircraft missiles guidance and firing systems and Nike Hercules guidance systems and Corporal missiles and Honest John missiles and Q-10 radar and TPS-25 radar and Redstone missiles . . .

All to make men spin and fall.

And, finally, they sent him to nuclear warhead school, where they were locked in a room with a civilian who chain-smoked so much even his pocket protector was stained as yellow as his teeth, and he showed them the ultimate weapon. The weapon itself was the size of a softball and the civilian told them if it were fired Correctly . . .

Used that word: 'Correctly'. Clipped the word so it was obviously capitalized in his brain.

. . . if you fired the weapon Correctly it would take out a whole city. Civilian had a little smile. As if he were slightly embarrassed at what he said. About taking out a whole city.

And the boy thought: Jesus.

Almost but not quite a prayer.

Thought: Jesus.

Make a whole city spin and fall.

From the schools, he went out into units and fixed computers and fired missile after missile and towards the end of his three-year enlistment they made him, of all things, a sergeant. Not like Sergeant Grim, same rank, but not training combat soldiers. An expert sergeant with technical weapons, fulfilling his destiny as the technical army's wet dream.

Yet even then, as a sergeant, he had not changed completely. Had not come out of the cocoon of his youth until they assigned him to Fort Bliss, Texas, where he was to help train other men in the use of high technical weapons to make even larger masses of people spin and fall.

Here the change finally came.

There were old men, in their late thirties and early forties, men who had fought in the Second World War and Korea and stayed in the army as a career. Men who were close to retiring, and while Vietnam was beginning to boil over and some of them would be killed there, that had not happened yet and they wanted to increase their technical knowledge, make their rank higher so they would get more money in retirement. Twenty more dollars a month. Maybe fifty dollars more a month.

But many of them, most of them, were poorly educated, had been drafted from rough places where they had to work as children and couldn't be in a school or a library, and had trouble with the classes.

They were assigned to old, enormous cavalry barracks, and the boy was there and they asked him to help them pass their tests and he said he would, tried to help them. When the boy was not working with them, many of them stayed in the barracks at night and played nickel-and-dime poker on blankets on top of trunks and drank clear alcohol out of jars.

And the boy, who was a sergeant but not of them, not like them, sat and watched them sitting in their underwear playing cards and drinking slowly, very professionally, out of quart jars, and the boy saw their scars.

Physical scars from wounds but more, many more scars in their spirits, scars that would never go away, as if the core of them, the centre of their being, had spun and fallen so that part of them was dead and would always be dead and they could never be more than what they had been when they were first scarred. Would never grow.

And he did not want that.

He wanted to grow and be more and do more than just that, sit by a trunk drinking clear liquid out of a jar talking in low sounds about battles long gone, long fought.

He could not be like them, nor could he be only his past; he wanted to see ahead, see what was over the next hill, and when he saw what was there, he wanted to keep going, see the next and the next and the next.

So he did.

No longer a boy, he lived and filled the years and saw

thousands of hills and oceans and forests and mountains and cities and some ugliness and much more beauty and people, God, all the people until finally, at last he came of an age, an old age, a still older age.

Eighty years.

Eighty glorious years absolutely packed with life.

And one day, living in a shack in the New Mexico mountains, he looked in an old box of things from his life, from moving, and saw one of the old blue Scripto notebooks that had somehow followed him in his life. And he picked up the notebook and opened it and found it was the story of the deer killed by hunters that he had written for the librarian.

But more, still more, there were empty pages after the story. Discoloured, but he could still see the lines, the beautiful lines that still, after all these years, called to him, dared him, and he sat down and found a pencil and thought:

What the hell.

Might as well write something down.

ABOUT THE AUTHOR

Gary Paulsen is the winner of the ALA Margaret Edwards Award for his contribution to young adult literature, and he is a three-time Newbery Honor winner for *Hatchet*, *Dogsong*, and *The Winter Room*. He lives in New Mexico.